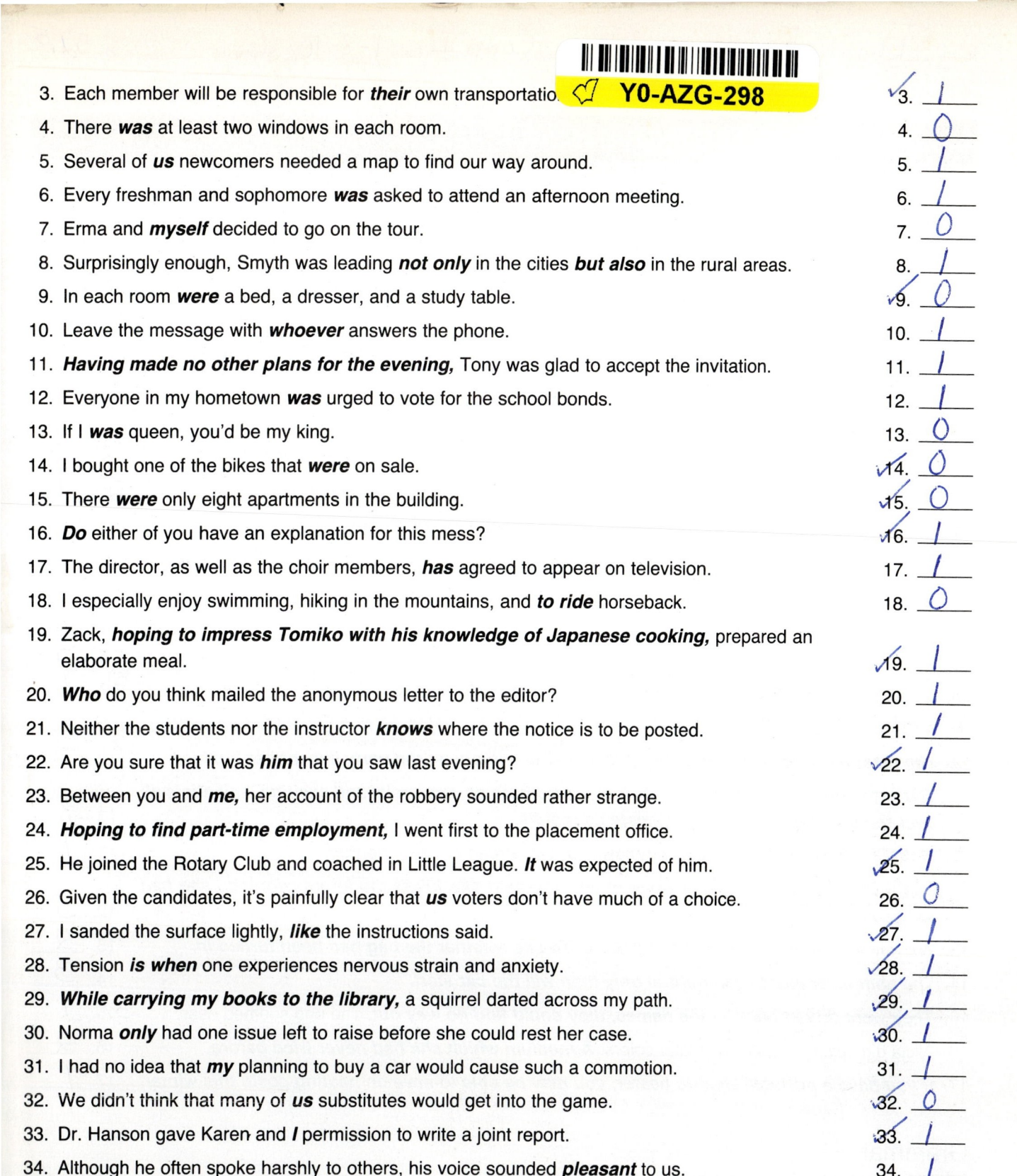

3. Each member will be responsible for *their* own transportation. 3. 1
4. There *was* at least two windows in each room. 4. 0
5. Several of *us* newcomers needed a map to find our way around. 5. 1
6. Every freshman and sophomore *was* asked to attend an afternoon meeting. 6. 1
7. Erma and *myself* decided to go on the tour. 7. 0
8. Surprisingly enough, Smyth was leading *not only* in the cities *but also* in the rural areas. 8. 1
9. In each room *were* a bed, a dresser, and a study table. 9. 0
10. Leave the message with *whoever* answers the phone. 10. 1
11. *Having made no other plans for the evening,* Tony was glad to accept the invitation. 11. 1
12. Everyone in my hometown *was* urged to vote for the school bonds. 12. 1
13. If I *was* queen, you'd be my king. 13. 0
14. I bought one of the bikes that *were* on sale. 14. 0
15. There *were* only eight apartments in the building. 15. 0
16. *Do* either of you have an explanation for this mess? 16. 1
17. The director, as well as the choir members, *has* agreed to appear on television. 17. 1
18. I especially enjoy swimming, hiking in the mountains, and *to ride* horseback. 18. 0
19. Zack, *hoping to impress Tomiko with his knowledge of Japanese cooking,* prepared an elaborate meal. 19. 1
20. *Who* do you think mailed the anonymous letter to the editor? 20. 1
21. Neither the students nor the instructor *knows* where the notice is to be posted. 21. 1
22. Are you sure that it was *him* that you saw last evening? 22. 1
23. Between you and *me,* her account of the robbery sounded rather strange. 23. 1
24. *Hoping to find part-time employment,* I went first to the placement office. 24. 1
25. He joined the Rotary Club and coached in Little League. *It* was expected of him. 25. 1
26. Given the candidates, it's painfully clear that *us* voters don't have much of a choice. 26. 0
27. I sanded the surface lightly, *like* the instructions said. 27. 1
28. Tension *is when* one experiences nervous strain and anxiety. 28. 1
29. *While carrying my books to the library,* a squirrel darted across my path. 29. 1
30. Norma *only* had one issue left to raise before she could rest her case. 30. 1
31. I had no idea that *my* planning to buy a car would cause such a commotion. 31. 1
32. We didn't think that many of *us* substitutes would get into the game. 32. 0
33. Dr. Hanson gave Karen and *I* permission to write a joint report. 33. 1
34. Although he often spoke harshly to others, his voice sounded *pleasant* to us. 34. 1
35. Neither the librarian nor the students in the reference room *was* aware of the situation. 35. 0
36. Professor Rogers looks very *differently* since he shaved his beard. 36. 0
37. There is no question that it was *she* behind the curtain. 37. 0
38. She had always been more ambitious scholastically than *he.* 38. 0
39. Dr. Smith, together with thirty of his students, *are* going on a field trip. 39. 1

Name: Tammy Francisco   Class: Comp II   Date: 1-8-90   Score (R ___ × 2) 52.5

1. DIAGNOSTIC TEST: GRAMMAR

Sentences

In the blank after each item,

> write **1** if the boldface expression is **one complete sentence**;
> write **2** if it is a **fragment** (incorrect: less than a complete sentence);
> write **3** if it is a **comma splice** or **fused sentence** (incorrect: two or more sentences written as one; also known as a **run-on**).

Example: Thoreau spent the night in jail. **Having refused to pay his taxes.**   2

1. Sylvia had brought her music. **But no one asked her to sing.**   1. 2
2. Packard was happy to retire. **His appetite for power completely sated.**   ②2. 1
3. I tried to enter the storeroom. **The door was stuck I could not force it open.**   3. 3
4. The Yankees made two big trades after the season had begun. **First for a shortstop and then for a center fielder.**   ②4. 1
5. The group made Morgan treasurer. **A job that appealed to him.**   5. 2
6. **The weather improved about noon, we went for a walk on the beach.**   6. 3
7. She drove up in a Wombat. **A small foreign car with huge headlights.**   ②7. 1
8. **Although Corey first had wanted to become a physics major, he finally decided on biology.**   8. 1
9. **The reason for her shyness being that she knew no one at the party except her hostess.**   ②9. 3
10. **The experiment to produce nuclear fusion was both controversial and exciting, scientists all over the world attempted to duplicate its results.**   10. 3
11. **Moberg learned too late that the typewriter had already been invented.**   11. 1
12. She revealed a surprising knowledge of art. **She said she loved the impressionists, she had studied them in Paris.**   12. 3
13. We walked over to the lost-and-found office. **To see whether the bag had been turned in.**   13. 2
14. **The shift lever must be in neutral only then will the car start.**   14. 3
15. **They were driven back by the flames, they could find no way out.** The end seemed near.   ③15. 1
16. Alicia did several pictures in water colors. **A medium which she had never tried before.**   16. 2
17. **If you have a portable electric heater, you may be able to save on heating costs this winter.**   17. 1

Grammar

In the blank after each sentence,

> write **1** if the boldface expression is used **correctly**;
> write **0** if it is used **incorrectly**.

Example: There **is** just three shopping days before Christmas.   0

1. The gendarmes assured Robert and **I** that our papers were in order.   ✓1. 1
2. Bill was fired from his new job, **which** made him despondent.   ✓2. 1

1

EXERCISES TO ACCOMPANY

English Simplified

EXERCISES TO ACCOMPANY

English Simplified

Sixth Edition

Blanche Ellsworth

**Revised by
Arnold Keller**
Vanier College

1817
HARPER & ROW, PUBLISHERS, New York
Grand Rapids, Philadelphia, St. Louis, San Francisco,
London, Singapore, Sydney, Tokyo

Sponsoring Editor: Lucy Rosendahl
Project Editor: Carla Samodulski
Art Direction: Lucy Krikorian
Cover Coordinator: Mary Archondes
Text and Cover Design: Brand X Studio/Robin Hoffman
Production: Paula Roppolo

Exercises to Accompany English Simplified, Sixth Edition

Copyright © 1990 by Harper & Row, Publishers, Inc.

All rights reserved. Printed in the United States of America. No part of this book may be used or reproduced in any manner whatsoever without written permission, except in the case of brief quotations embodied in critical articles and reviews. For information address Harper & Row, Publishers, Inc., 10 East 53d Street, New York, NY 10022.

ISBN 0–06–041917–2

89 90 91 92   9 8 7 6 5 4 3 2 1

CONTENTS

Preface vii

Diagnostic Tests
1. Grammar 1
2. Punctuation 4
3. Mechanics, Spelling, Usage 7

Grammar
4. Parts of a Sentence 10
5. Parts of Speech 12
6. Parts of Speech 13
7. Parts of Speech and Their Uses 14
8. Complements 16
9. Complements 17
10. Noun and Pronoun Use 18
11. Noun, Pronoun, and Adjective Use 19
12. Verb Tense 20
13. Verbs—Kind, Voice, and Mood 22
14. Verbals 24
15. Adjectives and Adverbs 25
16. Adjectives and Adverbs 27
17. Pronouns—Kind and Case 28
18. Pronoun Case 29
19. Pronoun Reference 32
20. Phrases 33
21. Verbal Phrases 35
22. Phrases—Review 37
23. Clauses 39
24. Clauses 41
25. Noun and Adjective Clauses 42
26. Adverb Clauses 43
27. Kinds of Sentences 44
28. Agreement—Subject and Verb 46
29. Agreement—Subject and Verb 48
30. Agreement—Pronoun and Antecedent 50
31. Agreement—Review 52
32. Fragments 53
33. Comma Splices and Fused Sentences 55
34. Fragments, Comma Splices, and Fused Sentences 56
35. Sentence Effectiveness 58
36. Parallel Structure 60
37. Parallel Structure 61
38. Placement of Modifiers 62
39. Dangling Modifiers 63
40. Dangling Modifiers 64
41. Review 65

Punctuation
42. The Comma 68
43. The Comma 70
44. The Comma 71
45. The Comma 72
46. The Comma 74
47. The Comma 76
48. The Period, Question Mark, and Exclamation Point 78
49. The Semicolon 79
50. The Semicolon and the Comma 80
51. The Semicolon and the Comma 82
52. The Apostrophe 84
53. The Apostrophe 85
54. The Apostrophe 86
55. Italics 88
56. Quotation Marks 90
57. Quotation Marks 92
58. Italics and Quotation Marks 94
59. The Colon, the Dash, Parentheses, and Brackets 96
60. The Hyphen 98
61. Review 99
62. Review 101

Mechanics
63. Capitals 103
64. Capitals 104
65. Numbers and Abbreviations 105
66. Capitals, Numbers, and Abbreviations 107

Spelling
67. Recognizing Correct Forms 109
68. Correcting Errors 112
69. Correcting Errors 114
70. Words Frequently Misspelled 116

Usage
71. Words Similar in Sound 118
72. Words Similar in Sound 120
73. Word Choice 123
74. Word Choice 125
75. Word Choice 126
76. Word Choice 128
77. Word Choice 130
78. Word Choice 131

Beyond the Sentence
79. Paragraph Development 132
80. Paragraph Development with Specifics 134
81. Paragraph Unity 135
82. Paragraph Coherence—Transitions 136
83. Bibliographic Form 137

Achievement Tests
84. Grammar 138
85. Punctuation 141
86. Mechanics, Spelling, Usage 144
87. Documentation 147

A List of Grammatical Terms 149

Teaching-Learning Aid: Diagraming 151

PREFACE

The sixth edition of *Exercises to Accompany English Simplified* preserves the spirit and form of earlier ones. The *Exercises* continue to offer practice in the comprehensive range of topics that is the hallmark of the *English Simplified* text. However, this latest volume also provides hundreds of new examples and sentences that reflect changing student populations and contemporary interests. Many exercises also ask students to respond more fully than in earlier editions; this should help instructors identify what students know and what they don't. Other new features include a brief glossary of terms and a convenient index to the *English Simplified* text; both should make it easier for students to find what they need.

A book like this has two main purposes: to help students become aware of language habits that may limit their performance and, by pinpointing errors, to help students correct them. No workbook can provide enough exercises to neutralize habitual errors; nor can a workbook itself ensure that students will transfer what they learn to their own essays. But a workbook can inform and guide students toward the practice and expectations of educated users of English.

An exercise that lets students guess at the right answer is unlikely to be effective. Throughout this workbook, therefore, we stress the need to know *why* a particular form is correct. Students typically must furnish not only right answers but the reasons for their choices. These techniques come from our own experiences in the classroom over more than four decades of teaching at San Francisco State University and at Vanier College. Indeed, we have drawn many of the sentences from student papers so as to represent the most frequently made errors.

Blanche Ellsworth
Arnold Keller

40. Each of the students **were** deserving of an opportunity to run for office.   40. _0_
41. **Hilda's** taking a part-time position meant that she had to budget her time carefully.   41. _0_
42. **Standing motionless on that windswept, dreary plain,** the rain pelted my face.   42. _1_
43. I had agreed to **promptly and without delay** notify them of my decision.   43. _1_
44. The dean agreed to award the scholarship to **whomever** the committee selected.   44. _0_
45. **Knowing that I should study,** it seemed wise for me not to go to the game.   45. _1_
46. **Who** were you trying to find in the auditorium yesterday?   46. _1_
47. The noise and the general chaos caused by the alarm **were** disturbing to the visitor.   47. _0_
48. As much as I would like to, I'll never be taller than **her.**   48. _1_
49. Only one of these stamps **is** of real value.   49. _1_
50. The guide showed Carol and **myself** all the main points of interest.   50. _0_

Name: Tammy Francisco   Class: Comp II   Date: 1-8-90   Score (R ___ × ½) 76.5

2. DIAGNOSTIC TEST: PUNCTUATION

In the blank after each sentence,

write **1** if the punctuation in brackets is **correct**;
write **0** if it is **incorrect**.
(Use only one number in each blank.)

Example: Regular exercise and sound nutritional habits[,] are essential for good health.   0

Example: Mr[.] Eliot worked in a bank.   1

1. Modern writers are often directly and profoundly influenced by the past[;] in fact, we can't fully study their work without knowing the traditions they draw on.   1. 1
2. A good horror movie doesn't merely scare us[,] but shows us worlds we never imagined.   2. 1
3. "Why can't a woman be more like a man["?] the chauvinist asked.   3. 0
4. I learned that the newly elected officers were Susie Fong, president[;] Leroy Jones, vice-president[;] Sandra Smith, treasurer[;] and Roger Douglas, secretary.   4. 1
5. The class expected low grades[. T]he test having been long and difficult.   5. 0
6. The puppy wagged it[']s tail excitedly.   6. 1
7. Eventually, everybody comes to *Rick's*[;] the best saloon in Casablanca.   7. 1
8. Louise's flight having been announced[,] she hurried to board the plane.   8. 1
9. We had misplaced our road map[,] we did not know which road to take.   9. 0
10. That is not the Sullivans' boat; at least, I think that it isn't their[']s.   10. 1
11. Since you've done reading the comic section[,] please pass it over to me.   11. 1
12. Inspector Trace asked, "Is that all you remember?[" "]Are you sure?"   12. 0
13. "The report is ready," Farnsworth said[,] "I'm sending it to the supervisor today."   13. 1
14. Didn't I hear you say, "I especially like blueberry pie"[?]   14. 0
15. Joe enrolled in a small college[;] although he had planned originally to attend a university.   15. 0
16. Stanley moved to Minneapolis[,] where he hoped to open a restaurant.   16. 1
17. That was a bit too close for comfort[,] wasn't it?   17. 1
18. The advertiser received more than two[-]hundred replies.   18. 1
19. Agnes is asking for two week[']s vacation to visit relatives in Canada.   19. 0
20. On April 7, 1976[,] the Citizens' Committee held a meeting in the Civic Auditorium.   20. 1
21. The womens['] basketball team has reached the quarter finals.   21. 1
22. I purchased several items[;] such as pencils, paper, a pen, and a notebook.   22. 1
23. She received twenty[-]three greeting cards on her sixtieth birthday.   23. 1
24. He hurried across the campus[,] and up the steps of the library.   24. 1
25. Many weeks before school was out[;] he had applied for a summer job.   25. 0
26. Dear Sir[;] Can you use an extra stock boy in your store this summer?   26. 0

4

27. Schweitzer summed up his ethics as "reverence for life[,]" a phrase which came to him during his early years in Africa.   27. _1_
28. We asked the custodian how many people the auditorium would hold[?]   28. _0_
29. "As for who won the election[—]well, not all the votes have been counted," she said.   29. _0_
30. Polly asked ["]if I had seen where she had put her glasses.["]   30. _1_
31. Any music[,] which is not jazz[,] does not appeal to him.   31. _0_
32. "Election results are coming in quickly now," the newscaster announced[;] "and we should be able to predict the winner soon."   32. _1_
33. The gates are locked[,] therefore, we shall have to visit the museum some other day.   33. _1_
34. The children went to the zoo[;] bought ice-cream cones[;] fed peanuts to the elephants[;] and watched the seals perform their tricks while being fed.   34. _0_
35. The camp director said, "The children like to sing ["]For He's a Jolly Good Fellow.["]"   35. _0_
36. Eleanor, who is a high-school senior, plans to be a nurse[;] but Adele, who is a college junior, wants to be a doctor.   36. _1_
37. *Sesame Street* is produced by the Childrens['] Television Workshop.   37. _1_
38. I shall go to the picnic[,] if someone offers me transportation.   38. _0_
39. Because he had watched a late show on television[,] he failed to hear his alarm clock.   39. _1_
40. Because of showers in the afternoon[,] the game had to be postponed.   40. _1_
41. That distinguished gentleman wearing the gray suit[,] has represented us in Congress for twenty years.   41. _0_
42. The scholarship award went to Julia Brown, the student[,] who had the highest grades.   42. _0_
43. The custodian was carrying[:] a broom, a dustpan, and a mop.   43. _0_
44. Elsie soon found that all the foods[,] which she especially liked[,] were high in calories.   44. _0_
45. Esther Greenberg[,] who is my roommate[,] comes from a small town.   45. _1_
46. "Only two people hav[']ent completed the assignment," the teacher said.   46. _0_
47. The talk show host[,] irritated and impatient[,] cut off the caller who insisted he was calling from aboard a flying saucer.   47. _1_
48. She went shopping[,] her salary check having arrived in the afternoon mail.   48. _1_
49. A note under the door read: "Sorry you weren't in. The Emerson[']s."   49. _0_
50. His father wanted him to be a banker[,] he wanted to be a musician or an actor.   50. _0_
51. He chopped wood for the fireplace[;] he piled the logs on the hearth.   51. _1_
52. The movie did not sell many tickets[.] Because nobody wanted to watch a four-hour documentary about dry cleaning.   52. _0_
53. The two boys, not knowing their way in the city[;] asked for directions.   53. _0_
54. By saving her money[,] Laura was able to attend college.   54. _1_
55. To gain recognition as a speaker[;] he accepted all invitations to appear before civic groups.   55. _0_
56. Sue Allen[,] who is a sophomore[,] is chairman of the Rally Committee.   56. _1_
57. Any man[,] who still opens the car door for his date[,] might well be considered old-fashioned.   57. _0_
58. "Oh dear[,] I hope I'm not late," said Clarence.   58. _1_

59. "Now you have only one guess left!"[,] gloated Rumpelstiltskin. 59. __0__
60. While speaking, the club president never knew the moment[,] at which someone might interrupt him. 60. __0__
61. We considered going to a movie[,] when our classes were over. 61. __0__
62. The courthouse having burned to the ground[,] the townspeople undertook plans to replace it. 62. __1__
63. I visited a town[,] where my aunt and uncle had once lived. 63. __0__
64. She spent the summer in Hawaii[,] where she enjoyed swimming in the surf. 64. __1__
65. Having learned that she was eligible for a scholarship[,] she turned in her application. 65. __1__
66. The fact that he had not yet found a place to live[,] did not especially bother him. 66. __0__
67. Stand with your hips flush against the wall[,] then see how far forward you can bend without losing your balance. 67. __1__

Name: Tammy Francisco   Class: Comp II   Date: 1-8-90   Score (R 56 × 5/4) 70%

3. DIAGNOSTIC TEST: MECHANICS, SPELLING, USAGE

Capitalization

In each blank,

write **1** if the boldface word(s) **follow** the rules of capitalization;
write **0** if they **do not**.

Example: Edgar Allan Poe was born in **Boston**.   1
Example: She comes from my **City**.   0

1. All **Sophomores** must attend.   1. 0
2. My **high school** days were fun.   2. 1
3. He attends Taft **high school**.   3. 0
4. The **President** vetoed the bill.   4. 0
5. Harry decided to go to school in the **East**.   5. 0
6. She sent her **Mother** a gift.   6. 0
7. I failed **french** again.   7. 0
8. She is in France; **He** is at home.   8. 0
9. "Are you coming?" **she** asked.   9. 1
10. I love **Chinese** food.   10. 0
11. We saluted the **american** flag.   11. 1
12. Last **Summer** I worked in a store.   12. 0
13. My birthday was on **Friday**.   13. 1
14. I am enrolled in courses in **philosophy** and French.   14. 1
15. She went **north** for Christmas.   15. 1
16. Please, **Father**; it's early.   16. 0
17. My **Aunt Martha** came to visit.   17. 1
18. "Stop!" **shouted** the officer.   18. 1
19. Roger refused to be **Chairman** of the committee.   19. 0
20. "If possible," he said, **"Come** early."   20. 0

Abbreviations and Numbers

In each blank,

write **1** if the boldface abbreviation or number is used correctly;
write **0** if it is used **incorrectly**.

Example: I love **NY**.   0

1. **Six million** people died.   1. 1
2. He is now **9** years old.   2. 0
3. The show starts at **8 P.M.**   3. 1
4. Dana was born on May **1st**, 1970.   4. 1
5. The rent is **$325** a month.   5. 0
6. The interest comes to **12** percent.   6. 0
7. I need to talk to the **prof**.   7. 0
8. There are **nineteen** women in the club.   8. 1
9. **1988** was another bad year for farmers.   9. 0
10. I wrote a note to **Dr.** Levy.   10. 1
11. He works at the Swiss Import **Co.**   11. 1
12. She lives on Buchanan **Ave.**   12. 1
13. We consulted Eric Brown, **Ph.D.**   13. 1
14. Our appointment is at **4** o'clock.   14. 0
15. I slept only **3** hours last night.   15. 0

7

Spelling

In each sentence, **one** boldface word is **misspelled**; write its number in the blank.

Example: (1)*Its* (2)*too* late (3)*to* go.   1

1. It was a (1)*privilege* to visit the (2)*phychology* (3)*professor's* class.   1. 2
2. The (1)*superintendant* insisted on (2)*repetition* in the (3)*mathematics* class.   2. 1
3. The (1)*mischievous* child became less (2)*aggressive* after attending (3)*kindegarten*.   3. 1
4. She was (1)*optimistic* about the possibility of (2)*competition* in (3)*athletics*.   4. 1
5. She was (1)*embarrassed* because of (2)*occasionally* writing (3)*mispelled* words.   5. 1
6. Two (1)*laboratory* courses were (2)*reccomended* by the high school (3)*principal*.   6. 2
7. The anthropologist was (1)*sincerely* puzzled when told that the behavior she thought (2)*courteous* was (3)*sacreligious*.   7. 2
8. We decided to test her (1)*intelligence,* (2)*knowledge,* and (3)*persistance*.   8. 3
9. It was impossible to (1)*acommodate* every (2)*conceivable* request, but Margaret took all (3)*necessary* steps to please her guests.   9. 1
10. Because she was (1)*diligent,* she was (2)*dissatisfied* with other than (3)*excellant* grades.   10. 3
11. It's (1)*permissable* to (2)*criticize* such (3)*outrageous* behavior, isn't it?   11. 1
12. The film showed the (1)*wierd* behavior of Count Thrasos, a true (2)*villain* who went to any length to (3)*pursue* evil.   12. 1
13. It was (1)*definite* that he needed to (2)*acquire* a knowledge of (3)*grammer*.   13. 3
14. It had (1)*occurred* to me that the (2)*omission* might weaken our (3)*arguement*.   14. 3
15. It was (1)*apparent* that a (2)*separate* (3)*questionaire* would be necessary.   15. 2

Usage

In the blank after each sentence,

write **1** if the boldface expression is used **correctly**;
write **0** if it is used **incorrectly**.

Example: Sacramento is the state **capitol**.   0

1. Hers is different **than** mine.   1. 0
2. I'm not hurt; I'm **alright**.   2. 1
3. The plane began its **descent** for Newark.   3. 1
4. Audrey complains **considerably**.   4. 0
5. The boxes **lay** where I had put them.   5. 0
6. He was **somewhat** disturbed.   6. 1
7. We didn't play **good** in the last quarter.   7. 1
8. She is not **enthused** about geometry.   8. 0
9. The clock was **lying** on its side.   9. 0
10. No one predicted the **affects** of the bomb.   10. 1
11. He **could scarcely** walk.   11. 1
12. I dislike **those kind** of people.   12. 0
13. We are going to **canvas** money for the Christmas Fund.   13. 1
14. The lamp **sits** on a small table.   14. 0
15. The house was **already** rented.   15. 1
16. The **principal** spoke to the students.   16. 1
17. I **had ought** to learn to drive.   17. 0

8

18. I stayed **for a while** longer. 18. __0__
19. **Almost** everyone had left. 19. __1__
20. He made **less** mistakes than I did. 20. __1__
21. She **rarely ever** eats candy. 21. __0__
22. The package had **burst** open. 22. __1__
23. Mrs. Grundy **censured** so much of the play, it was unintelligible. 23. __1__

24. I shall not **accept** the offer. 24. __1__
25. **Irregardless** of the dense fog, I drove. 25. __0__
26. Six states **comprise** New England. 26. __0__
27. Data **are** now available. 27. __1__
28. **Being that** I was tired, I left. 28. __0__
29. I phoned **in regard to** employment. 29. __1__
30. I **ought to of** called you. 30. __0__

Name: Tammy Francisco   Class: Comp II   Date: 1-15-90   Score (R __17__ × 5) 85%

4. GRAMMAR: PARTS OF A SENTENCE

(Study G-1.)

One of the numbers beneath each sentence marks the point where the **complete subject** ends and the **complete predicate** begins. Write that number in the blank.

Example: Dwight's youngest sister was named Maya.   __2__
               1   2   3

1. The Statue of Liberty was restored and reopened in 1988.   1. __1__
          1   2   3
2. Many of the abandoned railroad stations of America and Canada have been restored for other uses.   2. __2__
              1   2   3
3. Both the Baltimore Colts and the St. Louis Cardinals moved to new cities in 1988.   3. __2__
           1   2   3
4. The inspired singing of the children's choir filled us with tears of joy.   4. __3__
    1   2   3   4
5. Word processors, with their power to make editing easy, allow writers to revise as often as they wish.   5. __2__ ✓
            1   2   3
6. I have never in my career seen such incompetence.   6. __3__ ✓
  1   2   3 4
7. Which of the two cars is working today?   7. __2__
    1   2 3   4
8. Rarely would she leave her apartment after his death. [*This inverted-word-order sentence, rewritten in subject-predicate order, becomes* She would rarely leave her apartment after his death.]   8. __1__
                                 1   2   3   4
9. Which of the two cars have you driven today? [*Rewritten in subject-predicate order:* You have driven which of the two cars today?]   9. __1__
                                                      1
10. When did the dean and the director of admissions decide on your acceptance? [*Rewritten in subject-predicate order:* The dean and the director of admissions did decide on your acceptance when?]   10. __3__
                               1   2   3 4   5

Write **1** if the boldface word is a **subject** (or part of a compound subject).
Write **2** if it is a **predicate** (verb).
Write **3** if it is a **complement** (or part of a compound complement).
(Use the first column for the first boldface word, the second column for the second.)

Example: **Wendell** played a great **game.**   1   3
         The **crew** of the ship **was** afraid.   1   2

1. **All** perform their tragic **play.**   1. __1__ __3__
2. Champion athletes **spend** much **time** training and competing.   2. __2__ __3__
3. **Time** and **tide** wait for no one.   3. __1__ __1__
4. Not many **ships** **dock** here lately.   4. __1__ __2__

10

5. **We** will reach the **dock** within three minutes.   5. _1_ _3_
6. The **Senate voted** unanimously against the appointment.   6. _1_ _2_
7. The clustered **lights** far below the plane were **cities.**   7. _1_ _3_
8. A beacon **lights** the **runway** for arriving planes at night.   ✓8. _2_ _3_
9. Often the consequences of failure in a career are personal **depression** and economic **hardship.**   9. _3_ _3_
10. **Have you** any plans for the weekend?   10. _2_ _1_

Name: Tammy Francisco   Class: Comp II   Date: 1-15-90   Score (R 44 × 2) 88%

5. GRAMMAR: PARTS OF SPEECH

(Study G-2. Also study G-3 through G-6.)

Write the number (**1 to 8**, from the list below) of the **part of speech** of each boldface word:

1. noun 3. verb 5. adverb 7. conjunction
2. pronoun 4. adjective 6. preposition 8. interjection

Example: Hawthorne wrote **stories**. ___1___

1. Molly is a **singer** in a band. 1. _1_
2. You must **replace** the alternator. 2. _3_
3. **She** invented a better mousetrap. 3. _2_
4. The new law affected **all**. 4. _2_
5. Robert felt **tired**. 5. _3_
6. She was **here** a moment ago. 6. _5_
7. The lot sells **new** and used cars. 7. _4_
8. The test was hard **but** fair. 8. _7_
9. Do you want fries **with** that? 9. _6_
10. **This** book is mine. 10. _4_
11. **This** is the car to buy. 11. _2_
12. She lives **across** the street. 12. _6_
13. Is this **your** book? 13. _2_
14. The book is **mine**. 14. _2_
15. He wants an **education**. 15. _1_
16. She looks **like** her mother. 16. _6_
17. He agreed to proceed **slowly**. 17. _5_
18. They **were sleeping** soundly at noon. 18. _3_
19. I found an **unusual** stone. 19. _4_
20. She is **unusually** talented. 20. _5_
21. **Everyone** joined in the protest. 21. _2_
22. The **synagogue** is a landmark. 22. _1_
23. Students from all parts of the state **had come** to the rally. 23. _3_
24. The workers took a **strike** vote. 24. _4_
25. He is the one **whom** I suspect. 25. _2_

26. He whistles **while** he works. 26. _7_
27. What is your **plan**? 27. _1_
28. Nancy **is** a feminist. 28. _3_
29. No one came **after** ten o'clock. 29. _6_
30. Put the book **there**. 30. _5_
31. I saw him **once**. 31. _5_
32. The **theater** was dark. 32. _1_
33. He owns a **drugstore**. 33. _1_
34. Weren't **you** surprised? 34. _2_
35. They waited **for** us. 35. _6_
36. The oil spill was very **damaging**. 36. _3_
37. Did you pay your **dues**? 37. _1_
38. **All** survivors were calm. 38. _2_
39. **All** were calm. 39. _2_
40. The child slept **quietly**. 40. _5_
41. She **became** an executive. 41. _3_
42. **Well,** what shall we do now? 42. _8_
43. He worked **during** the summer. 43. _6_
44. **Tomorrow** is her birthday. 44. _5_
45. Will she call **tomorrow**? 45. _5_
46. **If** I go, will you come? 46. _7_
47. Leo hid **behind** the curtain. 47. _6_
48. He **should** never have been advanced in rank. 48. _3_
49. He drives **fast**. 49. _5_
50. Iris arrived at the park **early**. 50. _5_

12

Name: Tammy Francisco Class: Comp II Date: 1-15-90 Score (R 39 × 2) 78%

6. GRAMMAR: PARTS OF SPEECH

(Study G-2. Also study G-3 through G-6.)

Write the number (**1 to 8,** from the list below) of the **part of speech** of each boldface word:

1. noun   **3.** verb   **5.** adverb   **7.** conjunction
2. pronoun   **4.** adjective   **6.** preposition   **8.** interjection

Example: *Emilio* planned to become a surgeon.   1

1. *Clarify* what you mean. — 3
2. The letter should arrive *today*. — 1 (5)
3. *What* is the object of the game? — 2
4. She *never* confides in anyone. — 5
5. *May* I *call* you early on Friday? — 3
6. *Stately* trees surrounded the mansion. — 4
7. She enjoys tennis *and* boating. — 7
8. They *are* business associates. — 3
9. *Which* is your locker? — 2
10. Write to me *when* you can. — 5 (7)
11. *He* cannot believe her reply. — 2
12. *Neither* of the candidates spoke. — 2
13. *The* journey proved quite hazardous. — 4
14. The journey proved *quite* hazardous. — 5
15. With a few more votes, Hansen *would have been elected*. — 3
16. *Ah,* I thought you would agree. — 8
17. She spoke with genuine *feeling*. — 1
18. Mr. Wilson *is* a registered pharmacist. — 3
19. The jury decided that there was *criminal* intent. — 5 (4)
20. She *is painting* their house. — 3
21. *Maple* trees in Vermont are threatened by acid rain. — 4
22. He objected *strenuously*. — 5
23. This plane goes *to* Omaha. — 6
24. He is a real *diplomat*. — 1

25. *Unless* you qualify, you will be unable to compete. — 5 (7)
26. Emily stood *motionless*. — 5
27. Emily seemed in perpetual *motion*. — 1
28. Give the report to either Henry *or* Fred. — 7
29. The child was very *irritable*. — 5 (4)
30. Do you recognize *this* name? — 1 (4)
31. *Somebody* will surely notify you. — 2
32. She lives *on* a ranch in Idaho. — 6
33. The motive for the crime will *soon* become clear. — 3 (5)
34. *This* is a thankless task. — 2
35. *Accept* her offer without delay. — 3
36. I arrived *too* late to see him. — 5
37. Everybody talks *about* the weather. — 6
38. The child spoke *hesitantly*. — 5
39. You are *now* approaching Paris. — 5
40. The car was not new, but *it* was in good condition. — 2
41. *Roth* never published a second novel. — 1
42. He *has* always *liked* good food. — 3
43. We plan to make *an* early start. — 5 (4)
44. I want an *up-to-date* directory. — 4
45. Sit *between* Lois and me. — 5 (6)
46. The rug *should have been sent* to us three days ago. — 3
47. He fell *because* he was dizzy. — 7
48. *None* of the students failed. — 2
49. Van began to play *beautifully*. — 4 (5)
50. Supplies were *not* available. — 3 (5)

13

Name: Tammy Francisco Class: Comp II Date: 1-15-90 Score (R 30 x 2) 60%

7. GRAMMAR: PARTS OF SPEECH AND THEIR USES

(Study G-2 through G-6.)

In the first column, write the number (**1** to **8**, from the list below) of the **part of speech** of each boldface word.
In the second column, write the number (**9** to **25**, from the list) that tells how the word is used:

1. noun
2. pronoun
- 9. subject
- 10. direct object
- 11. indirect object
- 12. subjective complement
- 13. objective complement
- 14. object of preposition

3. verb
- 15. predicate

4. adjective
- 16. modifying noun or pronoun
- 17. subjective complement
- 18. objective complement

5. adverb
- 19. modifying verb
- 20. modifying adjective
- 21. modifying adverb

6. preposition
- 22. introducing prepositional phrase

7. conjunction
- 23. coordinating: joining words, phrases, or clauses of equal rank
- 24. subordinating: introducing dependent clause

8. interjection
- 25. showing emotion

	Part of Speech	Use		Part of Speech	Use
Example: The *Trojans* were defeated.	1	9	15. The *repetition* gets boring after a while.	1	10 ⑨
1. You *expect* me to believe that?	3	15	16. Lunch was just *soup*.	1	12
2. She is a tennis *star*.	2 ①	12	17. He drives *carefully*.	5	19
3. *What!* It can't be true!	8	25	18. He took her *advice*.	① 5	19 ⑩
4. *Green* creatures live there.	4	16	19. Your cousin is *on* the run.	6	22
5. Give *them* directions to Boise.	2	11	20. Up the trail came *Jim*.	1	10 ⑨
6. He seems *unfriendly*.	4	17	21. We rented *a* car.	4	17 ⑯
7. No one came with *me*.	2	11 ⑭	22. She was poor *but* dishonest.	7	23
8. Aren't *these* your keys?	2	10 ⑨	23. The path was *muddy*.	4	16 ⑰
9. Her son looks *like* her.	6	22	24. She looks *good* in red.	5 ④	19 ⑰
10. *Whom* did your friend see?	2	11 ⑩	25. I was *too* surprised to answer.	5	20
11. The voters elected Bush *president*.	1	13	26. Repeat the first *step*.	1	10
12. *Oh*, so that's it!	8	25	27. *Who* is afraid of them?	2	10 ⑨
13. He does *well* in tests.	⑤ 3	15 ⑭	28. Isn't *this* the street?	2	10 ⑨
14. She spoke *very* slowly.	5	21	29. He played *very* well.	5	21
			30. *Since* he was late for class, he ran.	7	24

14

31. **Look** at the flags!
32. The governor gave **Thompson** an order.
33. He ran **quickly**.
34. **"Hurrah!"** we yelled.
35. The stranger seemed unusually **hesitant**.
36. **Has** he **called** yet?
37. She is very **generous**.
38. **Biology** is her major.
39. **Hey,** that's my sandwich!
40. **Everyone** went to the rally except me.

31. 3 15
32. 1 11
33. 5 19
34. 8 25
35. 4 16 ⑰
36. 3 15
37. 4 17
38. 1 10
39. 8 25
40. 2 9

41. He seems **truly** sorry.
42. Yes, I **saw** her standing there.
43. It was a **silly** remark.
44. She asked **about** a job.
45. **Which** will be selected?
46. Will you tell him, **or** shall I?
47. The mayor declared the mall **open**.
48. His chances seem **good**.
49. Iron **and** zinc are metals.
50. The current was **swift**.

41. ⑤ ㉒ 4 18
42. 3 15
43. 4 18 ⑯
44. 6 22
45. 2 11 ⑫
46. 7 23
47. 4 18
48. ④5 19 ⑰
49. 7 23
50. 4 16 ⑰

Name: Tammy Francisco Class: Comp II Date: 1-29-90 Score (R 45 × 2) 90%

8. GRAMMAR: COMPLEMENTS

Can't have #2 if there isn't a #1.

(Study G-3.2B.)

Write the number that tells how the boldface complement **is used**:

AV 1. direct object   LV 3. subjective complement
   2. indirect object   4. objective complement

Example: Alex and Mallory took the **car**. 1

1. He has been an **environmentalist** for thirty years. 1. 3
2. This milk smells **sour**. 2. 3
3. We gave the **car** a shove. 3. 2
4. He is writing his **memoirs**. 4. 1
5. They elected Luella **head** of the committee. 5. 4
6. How can something taste **"light"**? 6. 3
7. Is he to be a **candidate**? 7. 3
8. Please give **me** your address. 8. 2
9. Alaska made Juneau its **capital**. 9. 4
10. She lent me a **map** of Warsaw. 10. 1
11. Give **me** your solemn promise. 11. 2
12. She built her own hi-fi **set**. 12. 1
13. She sounds **happier** every day. 13. 3
14. He brings his **lunch** with him. 14. 1
15. The university offered **her** an opportunity to do research. 15. 2
16. He has my best **wishes**. 16. ④ 4
17. She is a talented **actress**. 17. 3
18. Hamlet thought his mother **frail**. 18. 4
19. Pamela won a **scholarship**. 19. 1
20. Have you sent **copies** of the minutes to the members? 20. 1
21. **Whom** did you meet yesterday? 21. 1
22. Who designed the **plaque**? 22. 1
23. She is a **sophomore** now. 23. 3
24. Will you give **me** a chance? 24. 2
25. The sun on my back felt **good**. 25. ③ 4
26. Politicians will promise **us** anything. 26. 2

27. She gave me no **chance** to object. 27. ① 4
28. She is writing an **editorial**. 28. 1
29. They have been studying **Greek** for a semester. 29. 1
30. She has been earning **money** ever since she was eleven years old. 30. 1
31. Either she or I will call **you**. 31. 1
32. I gave **him** my coin collection. 32. 2
33. His objection sounded **foolish**. 33. ③ 4
34. **Which** did she choose? 34. 1
35. I named him my **beneficiary**. 35. 4
36. Were they the state **champions** last year? 36. 3
37. She is a **professor** at the local community college. 37. 3
38. She gave **me** no clue regarding her identity. 38. 2
39. That will be **all**, Hudson. 39. ③ 1
40. I made an **appointment** with my new adviser. 40. 1
41. She became an **administrator**. 41. 3
42. I agreed to consider his **offer**. 42. 1
43. He considered her a **genius**. 43. 4
44. Choose your **weapons** carefully, gentlemen. 44. 1
45. The company made her **manager** of the branch office. 45. 4
46. Wasn't that **unfortunate** about Aunt Sally? 46. 3
47. Give **me** the key to your office. 47. 2
48. She likes **opera and ballet**. 48. 1
49. He tends to be **irresponsible** at times. 49. 3
50. He decided to give the rowboat a **coat** of red paint. 50. 1

16

Name: Tammy Francisco   Class: Comp II   Date: 1-29-90   Score (R 42 x 2) 84%

9. GRAMMAR: COMPLEMENTS

(Study G-3.2B.)

Write the number that tells how the boldface complement **is used**:

1. direct object
2. objective complement (noun)
3. objective complement (adjective)
4. subjective complement (noun)
5. subjective complement (pronoun)
6. subjective complement (adjective)

Example: Hana is a **nurse**.   4

1. Anne received an anonymous **letter**.   1. 1
2. Jo was **dejected** after the loss.   2. 6
3. We considered Hal a **clown**.   3. 2
4. The music sounded **tuneless**.   4. 6
5. Wasn't that a great **dessert**?   5. 4
6. She named Santos her **assistant**.   6. 2
7. The judge declared him **insane**.   7. 3
8. Who threw out the first **pitch**?   8. 1
9. The dessert tasted **good**.   9. 6
10. Pat has been a **salesperson**.   10. 4
11. It was **he** who telephoned.   11. 1
12. Close the **door** quietly.   12. 1
13. The heat made us all **drowsy**.   13. 3
14. The experience was **unpleasant**.   14. 6
15. We met **them** backstage.   15. 1
16. The soup smelled very **good**.   16. 6
17. She is the construction **manager**.   17. 4
18. I consider her very **rude**.   18. 3
19. He recently bought a **ranch**.   19. 1
20. We elected her **treasurer**.   20. 2
21. This had been her **objective**.   21. 2
22. It is **we** who are responsible.   22. 1
23. Please leave the **key** with me.   23. 1
24. I denied that it was **I** who called.   24. 5
25. She studies **Russian** with a tutor.   25. 1
26. We consider her **honest**.   26. 3

27. **What** is the answer to the riddle?   27. 5
28. He has had great **recognition**.   28. 1
29. Daley had been **mayor** for many years.   29. 4
30. He did not seem particularly **worried**.   30. 1
31. She is **someone** you can trust.   31. 5
32. He enjoys **fishing** in the lake.   32. 1
33. She runs a **marathon** each year.   33. 1
34. June's hobby is **sculpture**.   34. 1
35. He must have been sound **asleep**.   35. 6
36. Alexandra has no **lack** of intelligence.   36. ___
37. Our interest in her career made her very **happy**.   37. 3
38. Was it **you** who wrote the essay?   38. 5
39. Did you find the **dictionary**?   39. 1
40. Are you the office **manager**?   40. 4
41. Is the victim **anyone** I know?   41. 5
42. Tyson defeated **everyone** who challenged him.   42. 1
43. The culprit was **neither** of the children originally suspected.   43. 3
44. His confidence was **shaken**.   44. 6
45. They made him a good **offer**.   45. 1
46. I appointed him **bailiff**.   46. 2
47. I appointed **him** bailiff.   47. 1
48. She usually felt **neglected**.   48. 6
49. She considers him **stupid**.   49. 3
50. Elliot convinced us **completely**.   50. 3

17

Name: Tammy Francisco   Class: Comp II   Date: 1-29-90   Score (R ___ × 4) ___

10. GRAMMAR: NOUN AND PRONOUN USE

(Study G-3 and G-6.)

Write the number that tells how each boldface noun or pronoun **is used**:
Use the first column for the first boldface word, the second column for the second.

1. subject
2. direct object
3. indirect object
4. subjective complement
5. objective complement
6. object of preposition
7. appositive
8. direct address

Example: The *Marines* stormed the *barricades*.   1: 1   2: 2

1. *Debris* from the *wreck* was strewn everywhere. — 2, 1 (1 circled)
2. Some of his fellow *officers* considered *Benedict* somewhat untrustworthy. — 6, 2
3. That must have been the *reason* that she told *us*. — 4/3, 2
4. His unorthodox behavior made *Singer* the *object* of criticism. — 2, 5
5. The CIA appointed *Huang* its chief Asian *agent*. — 2, 7/5
6. Dorothy, his *sister*, was with him when he revisited the *house*. — 7, 2/6
7. Down the library steps came *Anna*, her arms filled with reference *books*. — 1, 2/6
8. Having completed the test, she put her *paper* on the instructor's *desk* and left. — 2, 6
9. There are fourteen *students* whom the dean has named campus *assistants*. — 2, 5
10. Because she seemed genuinely interested, we told the *dean* our *troubles*. — 3/2, 4/2
11. *Pasadena* will again be the *site* of the Rose Bowl. — 1, 2/4
12. Having bought season *tickets*, I saw *most* of the Bears' games. — 2, 2
13. First read the *instructions*; then answer the *questions* carefully. — 2, 2
14. Although he knew the *answers* to most of the *questions*, he did not finish the test. — 2, 6
15. She gave each *student* an *opportunity* to try out for a part in the play. — 3, 2
16. It is, my fellow *students*, time for you to give *me* your close attention. — 8, 3
17. *He* thought about the *day* when he first met Cynthia. — 1, 2/6
18. The club *president* invited the members to suggest a *program* for the semester. — 1, 6/2
19. My Uncle Bruno has made *me* *vice-president* of his shoe factory. — 2, 5
20. General Grapeshot's unorthodox *tactics* bewildered the *enemy*. — 1/4, 2/5
21. Unless I am misinformed, she considers *herself* a *nonconformist*. — 2, 5
22. Dr. Ricardo promised *Gary* that the exam results would be *posted*. — 3, 4
23. There are, *ladies and gentlemen*, many *opportunities* to hear good speakers. — 8, 2/1
24. "Wasn't *he* invited?" asked *Hilda*, my roommate. — 1, 2/1
25. We asked the *speaker*, a former Olympic *medalist*, to speak on physical fitness. — 2, 5/7

18

Name _____ Class _____ Date _____ Score (R _____ × 10/3) _____

11. GRAMMAR: NOUN, PRONOUN, AND ADJECTIVE USE

(Study G-3, G-5, and G-6.)

out of 106
93 right
↑ to 3 includi
pg. 25

In the first column, write the number (**1** to **3**) of the **part of speech** of the boldface word:
In the second column, write the number (**4** to **9**) that tells how the word **is used**:

1. noun	4. subject	7. subjective complement
2. pronoun	5. direct object	8. objective complement
3. adjective	6. indirect object	9. object of preposition

(between verbs, DO)

	Part of Speech	Use		Part of Speech	Use
Example: Music filled the **air**.	1	5	16. Willy became **frightened** by all his failures.	16. ___ ___
1. I lent him some **money**.	1. 1	5	17. Will **someone** please help me?	17. ___ ___
2. **Mohammed** made the first team.	2. 1	4	18. The jury found him **guilty**.	18. ___ ___
3. I named **her** my successor.	3. 2	5	19. She tried to appear **poised**.	19. ___ ___
4. We elected him **secretary**.	4. 1	8	20. He has many **friends**.	20. ___ ___
5. Duncan has been a commercial **pilot** for ten years.	5. 1	7	21. She sent **everyone** a thank-you note.	21. ___ ___
6. The gift is for **her**.	6. 2	9	22. Her story sounds **plausible**.	22. ___ ___
7. He has been **eager** to visit this country.	7. 3	7	23. Is **this** your notebook?	23. ___ ___
8. I gave **Sofia** a book.	8. 1	6	24. Paolo removed the **books** from his locker.	24. ___ ___
9. Boris became a **chemist**.	9. 1	7	25. The results proved **interesting**.	25. ___ ___
10. The puppy seemed **timid** when he first arrived.	10. 3	7	26. **Neither** of us went.	26. ___ ___
11. The report is of interest to **us**.	11. ___ ___	27. Give **her** A for effort.	27. ___ ___
12. Jogging keeps her **healthy**.	12. ___ ___	28. He became an able **administrator**.	28. ___ ___
13. Give **us** a few good men.	13. ___ ___	29. Can you give **us** a hint?	29. ___ ___
14. Is **he** your cousin?	14. ___ ___	30. Few people today are afraid of **flying**.	30. ___ ___
15. She lives in **Detroit**.	15. ___ ___		

20 right

(15+10) 19

Name _____ Class ____ Date ____ Score (R ____ × 10/4) ____

12. GRAMMAR: VERB TENSE

(Study G-4.)

Write the number of the **tense** (time) of the boldface verb:

1. present   4. present perfect (*have* or *has*)
2. past   5. past perfect (*had*)
3. future (*shall* or *will*) 6. future perfect (*shall have* or *will have*)

Example: You **spoke** too soon.   2

1. The sun **sets** in the west.   1. 1
2. He **will** surely **write** us soon.   2. 3
3. Next summer, we **shall have lived** in this house for ten years. 3. 6
4. The Allens **have planted** a vegetable garden. 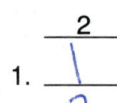 4. 2

5. By noon he **will have finished** the whole job. 5. 6
6. Here **is** the six o'clock news.   6. 1
7. **Shall** we **reserve** a copy for you? 7. 3
8. The widow's savings **melted** away.   8. 2
9. I **had** not **expected** to see her. 9. 5
10. Carol **sends** her love.   10. 1

In the blank at the right, write the number of the **verb ending**, if any, that should appear at each bracketed space:

0. no ending   1. *s* or *es*   2. *ed* or *d*   3. *ing*

Example: The sun rise[ ] beyond that low hill.   1

The brown cliffs rise[1] directly from the gray sea; no buffer beach come[2] between them. The waves have pound[3] the granite base of that cliff for ages but have fail[4] to wear[5] it away. Now, as always, great white gulls circle[6] just above the foam, seeking fish that are destine[7] to become their dinner. Years ago, when I first gather[8] the courage to approach[9] the cliff's sheer edge and peer[10] over, I imagine[11] what it would be like if I tumble[12] over and plummet[13] into that seething surf.

I was an imaginative youth, and the thought fascinate[14] me then. At that time I was try[15] desperately though unsuccessfully to win the heart of a dark-haired local girl, but she had been continually reject[16] me, and her attitude had turn[17] my thoughts to suicide. I might, in fact, have hurl[18] myself over the edge, except for one fact: My knees have always turn[19] to jelly at the mere thought of do[20] it.

Today, as a man of thirty, I can look[21] back on those years and laugh[22]. Yet even now, whenever I approach[23] that treacherous edge, a chill run[24] through me. It is as if something inside me is say[25]

1. 0
2. 1
3. 2
4. 2
5. 0
6. 0
7. 2
8. 2
9. 0
10. 2
11. 2
12. 2
13. 2
14. 2

20

"Someday you will hurl[26] yourself over. You know[27] it." I have been haunt[28] by that thought ever since that girl reject[29] me, and I probably will always be obsess[30] by it—until the end.

15. 3
16. 3
17. 2
18. 2
19. 2
20. 3
21. 0
22. 0
23. 0
24. 1
25. 3
26. 0
27. 0
28. 2
29. 2
30. 2

Name _____ Class _____ Date _____ Score (R _____ × 7/3) _____

13. GRAMMAR: VERBS—KIND, VOICE, AND MOOD

(Study G-4.)

Write **1** if the boldface verb is **transitive**. transfer action from one thing to another
Write **2** if it is **intransitive**. no action transferred *(subject to something else)*
Write **3** if it is a **linking** verb.

Example: The house *looks* fine.   __3__

1. Jenny *kissed* me when we met.   1. __1__
2. Gay *jogs* for two miles every morning.   2. __2__
3. Your laughter *sounds* bitter.   3. __2__
4. *Lay* your books on the table.   4. __1__
5. The window *opened* onto the bay.   5. __2__
6. Dr. Smiley *has* a fine reputation.   6. __3__ ✓ (circled)
7. The island *lay* fifty miles off the mainland.   7. __1__
8. The last express *has* already *left*.   8. __2__
9. Sue *lay* down for a short rest.   9. __1__
10. The childhood playmates *remained* friends for life.   10. __3__
11. The milk *smells* sour.   11. __2__
12. The directions *seem* simple enough.   12. __3__
13. The express *arrived* ten minutes late.   13. __2__

Write **1** if the boldface verb is in the **active** voice.
Write **2** if it is in the **passive** voice.

Example: Lefty *threw* another strike.   __1__

1. Visitors *are* not *permitted* aboard the aircraft.   1. ____
2. One name *was* inadvertently *omitted* from the list.   2. __2__
3. The conductor *can*not *make* change for passengers.   3. ____
4. Man *proposes*, God disposes.   4. __1__
5. The meeting *was called* to order.   5. ____
6. The ancient city *was* totally *destroyed* by a volcanic eruption.   6. __2__
7. An unfortunate error *has been made*.   7. ____
8. Stan *has found* the letter.   8. __1__
9. The witness *faltered* under the vigorous cross-examination.   9. ____
10. The robbery *could have occurred* about noon.   10. __2__ (circled)
11. The arms treaty *will be signed* next month.   11. ____
12. The left-fielder *threw out* the runner.   12. __2__
13. Jorge's credit card application *was approved*.   13. ____
14. Batman *will have been seen* by millions before the end of the summer.   14. __2__
15. The virus *was* susceptible to heat.   15. ____

Write the number of the **mood** of the boldface verb:

1. indicative   2. imperative   3. subjunctive

Example: If she *were* smart, she'd finish school first.   __3__

1. The semester *had ended*.   1. ____
2. They *are* cousins.   2. __1__
3. *Kiss* me, you fool!   3. ____
4. He *is building* a house.   4. __1__
5. Would that I *were* wealthy!   5. ____
6. *Send* my check to the bank.   6. __2__
7. If I *were* you, I'd not worry.   7. ____
8. *Stay* away from the cliff.   8. __2__
9. Rosa *offered* us some tea.   9. ____

22

4 ver

10. Please *thank* her for me.
11. I wish you *were* here.
12. They *were* late as usual.

10. 2
11. ___
12. 3

13. *Hurry!*
14. I *hurried* to get to home.
15. If this *be* treason, make the most of it.

13. ___
14. E
15. ___

out of 16 → 14 right

Name _____ Class _____ Date _____ Score (R ____ × 3) ____

14. GRAMMAR: VERBALS

(Study G-4 and G-7.2.)

Classify each **boldface** verbal:

1. infinitive 3. present participle
2. gerund   4. past participle

7 right

Example: *To be* or not be; that is the question. __1__

1. Do you like **to watch** football? 1. __1__
2. **Watching** the game, she grew bored. 2. __3__
3. His pastime is **watching** football. 3. __3__ (2)
4. The President's first job was **to restore** confidence. 4. __1__
5. She enjoys **winning** at chess. 5. __2__
6. This is a good plan **to follow**. 6. __1__
7. Our **talking** distracted him. 7. __2__
8. I submitted a **word-processed** essay. 8. __4__
9. **Frightened,** the seal pups retreated. 9. ____
10. She dislikes **barking** dogs. 10. ____
11. He was eager **to begin**. 11. ____
12. By **hurrying,** he caught the bus. 12. ____
13. **Seeing** us, she smiled. 13. ____

14. She enjoys **driving** sports cars. 14. ____
15. She objects to our **watching** her. 15. ____
16. Not **knowing** a soul, she was lonely. 16. ____
17. He spent too much time **watching** television. 17. ____
18. **Frightened,** he became cautious. 18. ____
19. Her plan is **to leave** early. 19. ____
20. **Amazed,** she began to laugh. 20. ____
21. The **frightened** children cried. 21. ____
22. **Swimming** is good exercise. 22. ____
23. **Hitting** Langston's fastball was impossible that day. 23. ____
24. Yours is not **to reason** why. 24. ____
25. **Reducing** carbon dioxide emissions was a top priority in the President's bill. 25. ____

In the first column, **classify** each boldface verbal:

1. infinitive 2. gerund

In the second column, write the number that tells how that verbal **is used**:

3. subject   5. subjective complement
4. direct object   6. object of preposition

Example: *Sleeping* until noon is no way to greet the day.   2   1

1. General Grapeshot always enjoyed **holding** surprise inspections. 1. __2__ ___
2. **To invent** a better mousetrap had been her childhood dream. 2. __1__ ___
3. Larry likes **working** with young children in summer camps. 3. __2__ ___
4. The ambassador's first task was **to arrange** a summit meeting. 4. __1__ ___
5. The suspect apparently had no intention of **admitting** the crime. 5. __2__ ___
6. Antonio worried about **borrowing** money. 6. __2__ ___
7. We tried **to stop** him from making an unwise decision. 7. __1__ ___
8. Her one wish has always been **to travel** extensively in Europe. 8. __1__ ___
9. **Writing** a letter of application was no problem for her. 9. __2__ ___

24

15. GRAMMAR: ADJECTIVES AND ADVERBS

(Study G-5.)

Write **1** if the boldface adjective or adverb is used **correctly**.
Write **0** if it is used **incorrectly**.

13 right

Example: The Cardinals are playing **good** this year.   0

1. That sun feels **good**.   1. 1
2. The team shouldn't feel **badly** about losing that game.   2. 0
3. She was the *more* **most talented** member of the pair.   3. 1 0
4. He keeps in **good** condition always.   4. 1
5. Speak **softly** and carry a big stick.   5. 0 1
6. He was very **frank** in his evaluation of her work.   6. 1
7. He spoke very **frankly** to us.   7. 0 1
8. Of the two girls, she is the **prettiest**.   8. 1 0
9. My head aches **bad**.   9. 0
10. The child looked **hungry**.   10. 1
11. The child looked **hungrily** at the food on the table.   11. 0 1
12. I comb my hair **different** now.   12. 1 0
13. Fleagle talks too **smooth** to be trusted.   13. 0
14. Was Alex hurt **bad**?   14. 1 0
15. He limps **considerably**.   15. 1
16. He seemed **real** honest.   16. 1 0
17. I told **most** everyone the news.   17. 1 0
18. The milk tasted **sour**.   18. 1
19. Do you intend to go to the concert tonight? **Sure**, I do.   19. 1 0
20. Reading John Irving is a **real** pleasure.   20. 1
21. The tamer glanced **nervously** at the angry tigers.   21. 1
22. The crowd seemed **nervous** also.   22. 1
23. The campus will look **differently** when the new buildings are completed.   23. _____
24. This is the **clearest** of the two explanations.   24. _____

25. The book is in **good** condition.   25. _____
26. I did **poor** in French this term.   26. _____
27. She always looks **good** in green.   27. _____
28. Ericson felt **badly** about having to fire the veteran employee.   28. _____
29. Daryl's excuse was far **more poorer** than Keith's.   29. _____
30. The attic smelled **musty**.   30. _____
31. She speaks very **well**.   31. _____
32. It rained **steady** for the whole month of June.   32. _____
33. The roses smell **sweet**.   33. _____
34. He tries **hard** to please everyone.   34. _____
35. The man shouted **loudly** at her.   35. _____
36. John is **near** seven feet tall.   36. _____
37. He talked **considerable** about his future plans.   37. _____
38. She donated a **considerable** sum of money to the project.   38. _____
39. The **smartest** of the twins is spoiled.   39. _____
40. The **smartest** of the triplets is spoiled.   40. _____
41. The coach looked **uneasily** at his players.   41. _____
42. He felt **uneasy** about the score.   42. _____
43. Do try to drive more **careful**.   43. _____
44. It was Bob's **most unique** idea ever.   44. _____
45. I knotted the rope **loosely**.   45. _____
46. Salisha arrived **considerable** later than the others.   46. _____
47. The street looked **strangely** to us.   47. _____
48. The child sounded **unhappy**.   48. _____
49. The car has run **good** since it was last repaired.   49. _____

25

15+/22

50. He was ill, but he is **well** now. 50. _____
51. This is the **cheapest** of the two cars. 51. _____
52. The music sounded **good** throughout the hall. 52. _____
53. Bryant was **really** apologetic to Willard. 53. _____
54. Her dress looks **expensive.** 54. _____
55. Lonnie drives too **fast.** 55. _____
56. He seemed very **serious** about keeping his appointment. 56. _____
57. The stuffed cabbage smelled **good.** 57. _____
58. We felt **badly** about missing the farewell party. 58. _____
59. Barry looked on **sadly.** 59. _____
60. Barry was **sad** all morning. 60. _____

16. GRAMMAR: ADJECTIVES AND ADVERBS

(Study G-5.)

Write **1** if the boldface adjective is used **correctly**.
Write **0** if it is used **incorrectly**; then write the correction in the second column.

Example: He hit the ball **good**.	0	well
1. Carl is the **fastest** of the two sprinters.	1. 1	
2. The Orioles felt **badly** about their tenth loss.	2. 0	bad
3. We played **poor** for three quarters.	3. 0	poorly
4. The little ones look **real** sleepy to me, Mother.	4. 0	really
5. They play their music much, much too **loudly**.	5. 1	
6. Of Lear's three daughters, Cordelia was the **younger**.	6. 0	youngest
7. Hulk thought **deep** for a while and then fell over.	7. 1	
8. **Uneasily** is the head that wears the crown.	8. 0	Uneasy
9. Her clothes are always **tasty**.	9.	
10. I am quite **well**, thank you.	10. 1	

Name _____ Class _____ Date _____ Score (R _____ × 4) _____

17. GRAMMAR: PRONOUNS—KIND AND CASE

(Study G-6.)

Classify each boldface pronoun:

1. personal pronoun   5. indefinite pronoun
2. interrogative pronoun   6. reciprocal pronoun
3. relative pronoun   7. reflexive pronoun
4. demonstrative pronoun   8. intensive pronoun

Example: *Who* is Sylvia?   2

1. I made him an offer that *he* could not refuse.   1. 1
2. *No one* expected the storm to last so long.   2. 5
3. *This* is another fine mess you've gotten us into!   3. 4
4. He has only *himself* to blame for his predicament.   4. 7
5. *Which* of the local high schools has the best football team?   5. 2
6. She is the executive *who* makes the key decisions in this company. 6. 3
7. I *myself* have no desire to explore the rough terrain of mountainous regions. 7. 8
8. The twins resembled *each other* in appearance and disposition.   8. 6
9. *Several* of the games went into overtime.   9. 5
10. Has *anyone* ever suggested that he might just be lazy?   10. 5
11. The five brothers depended on *one another* for moral support.   11. 6
12. These are my biology notes; *those* must be yours.   12. 4
13. *Who* do you think will be the successful candidate in the student-body election? 13. 2
14. *Each* of the hostages had begged to go home.   14. 8
15. *Neither* of the parties engaged in collective bargaining would budge from its position. 15. 5

Write the number of the **correct** pronoun choice.

Example: Grandpa ordered lunch for Billy and (1)*I* (2)*me.*   2

1. Three of (1)*we* (2)*us* jury members voted for acquittal.   1. 2
2. If you were (1)*I* (2)*me,* would you be willing to change your plans completely? 2. 2
3. May we—John and (1)*I* (2)*me*—join you for lunch in the cafeteria? 3. 1
4. Between you and (1)*I* (2)*me,* I feel quite uneasy about the outcome of the expedition. 4. 2
5. Were you surprised that the trophies were awarded to Julia and (1)*he* (2)*him?* 5. 2
6. It must have been (1)*they* (2)*them* who called on us last evening. 6. _____
7. Why not give (1)*we* (2)*us* students an opportunity to help determine the matter? 7. _____
8. Nobody but (1)*she* (2)*her* can answer that question.   8. _____
9. He is much more talented in dramatics than (1)*she* (2)*her.*   9. _____
10. The governor supported (1)*whoever* (2)*whomever* supported the governor. 10. _____

Name _____ Class _____ Date _____ Score (R _____ × ⅔) _____

18. GRAMMAR: PRONOUN CASE

(Study G-6.2.)   Pg 175

In the first column, write the number of the **correct** pronoun choice.
In the second column, write the number of the **reason** for your choice:

Choice

1. **subject form (nominative case)**   *subjects 3. subject complements*

2. **object form (objective case)**   *DO, IO, objects of Prep.*

Reason for Choice

{ 3. subject of verb
  4. subjective complement
  5. direct object
  6. indirect object
  7. object of preposition
  8. subject of infinitive }   ⑨

	Word Choice	Reason for Choice
Example: Marie studied with Burt and (1)*I* (2)*me*.	2	7
1. Rashid begged Betsy and (1)*I* (2)*me* to stay up late.	2	5 ⑧
2. Do you think it was (1)*she* (2)*her* who poisoned the cocoa?	1	3 ④
3. Were you and (1)*he* (2)*him* surprised by the result?	1	4 ③
4. Fourteen of (1)*we* (2)*us* students signed a petition to reverse the ruling.	2	7
5. The assignment gave (1)*she* (2)*her* no further trouble (after it was explained.)	2	6
6. She greeted, with great cordiality, the guests (1)*who* (2)*whom* I had brought. *DO*	2	5
7. Shall we give (1)*they* (2)*them* an opportunity to enter the speech competition?		
8. I invited (1)*he* (2)*him* to select topics on which students might speak easily.		
9. Girls like (1)*she* (2)*her* are something special.		
10. I was very much surprised to see (1)*he* (2)*him* at the art exhibit.		
11. Are you and (1)*he* (2)*him* both working in the school cafeteria this year?		
12. We asked Joan and (1)*he* (2)*him* to supervise the playground activities.		
13. She asked, "(1)*Who* (2)*Whom* is willing to take charge of the ticket sale?"		
14. The top students in the class were Charles and (1)*she* (2)*her*.		
15. All of (1)*we* (2)*us* freshmen were asked to report for an orientation session.		
16. It was (1)*he* (2)*him* who made all the arrangements for the dance.		
17. Give the scholarship money to (1)*whoever* (2)*whomever* has the highest grades.		
18. My two friends and (1)*I* (2)*me* decided to go on a boat ride around the bay.		
19. This argument is just between Dick and (1)*I* (2)*me*.		
20. My father always gave (1)*I* (2)*me* money for my tuition.		
21. My sister scolded (1)*I* (2)*me* for not writing to her more frequently.		
22. I expect to go to the picnic with (1)*whoever* (2)*whomever* asks me.		

㉙

1st 6

23. If you were (1)*I* (2)*me,* would you consider going on a summer cruise?
24. Please ask (1)*whoever* (2)*whomever* is at the door to wait.
25. (1)*Who* (2)*Whom* is the speaker to be at the noon assembly?
26. Everyone was excused from class except Louise, Mary, and (1)*I* (2)*me.*
27. The host asked (1)*he* (2)*him* to sing another chorus.
28. Florence is as capable as (1)*he* (2)*him* of typing the minutes of the meeting.
29. I knew of no one who had encountered more difficulties than (1)*she* (2)*her.*
30. Nobody but (1)*he* (2)*him* had been able to qualify for an overseas scholarship.
31. I hope to be the first to congratulate (1)*he* (2)*him* on his success.
32. The frisbee gently drifted toward Bonnie and (1)*I* (2)*me.*
33. The teacher asked (1)*we* (2)*us* to speak extemporaneously on the panel topic.
34. Her brother is ten years younger than (1)*she* (2)*her.*
35. Fifty of (1)*we* (2)*us* agreed to raise money for a memorial plaque.
36. The Kaplans offered (1)*she* (2)*her* a job for the summer.
37. Are you and (1)*she* (2)*her* planning to live in New Jersey?
38. Nobody but (1)*he* (2)*him* knows the combination to the school safe.
39. I had decided to ask (1)*he* (2)*him* to officiate at the ceremony.
40. My friends had refused to go on the excursion without (1)*I* (2)*me.*
41. I am certain that he is as deserving of praise as (1)*she* (2)*her.*
42. If you were (1)*I* (2)*me,* which courses would you select as electives?
43. (1)*Who* (2)*Whom* do you think will be the next mayor?
44. Assign the task to (1)*whoever* (2)*whomever* is willing to undertake it.
45. She is a person (1)*who* (2)*whom* is, without question, destined to achieve success.
46. He is the author about (1)*who* (2)*whom* we shall be writing a paper.
47. Was it (1)*he* (2)*him* who became an all-American football player?
48. The only choice left was between (1)*she* (2)*her* and him.
49. No one was critical of the performance but (1)*she* (2)*her.*
50. The instructor asked (1)*I* (2)*me* to appear on a panel with three of my classmates.
51. "Were you calling (1)*I* (2)*me*?" Jill asked as she entered the room.
52. Shouldn't we give (1)*she* (2)*her* an opportunity to state her opinion?
53. Marilyn and (1)*I* (2)*me* played the leads in *Romeo and Juliet* last year.
54. Both of (1)*we* (2)*us* agreed that the unaccustomed exercise had been too much for us.
55. Mr. Parker is probably a more competent editor than (1)*he* (2)*him* is a swimmer.
56. Imagine finally meeting (1)*he* (2)*him* after so many years of correspondence!
57. My mother asked one of the other tourists to photograph the twins and (1)*she* (2)*her* in front of the fountain.
58. Do you suppose that (1)*he* (2)*him* will ever find time to come?
59. Everyone at the lake except (1)*I* (2)*me* is an ardent fisher.

60. Everyone but (1)*she* (2)*her* was there on time. 60. _____ _____
61. It was known that the officials wanted Gina rather than (1)*she* (2)*her.* 61. _____ _____
62. The student (1)*who* (2)*whom* Dr. Potter asked to answer wasn't prepared. 62. _____ _____
63. It was Holmes who noticed the footprints on the ceiling, not (1)*I* (2)*me.* 63. _____ _____
64. Watching our team win the Super Bowl gave our friends and (1)*we* (2)*us* much satisfaction. 64. _____ _____
65. A dispute arose about (1)*who* (2)*whom* would pay the check. 65. _____ _____
66. She is the one (1)*who* (2)*whom* I am certain will win the award. 66. _____ _____
67. The scholarship will be given to (1)*whoever* (2)*whomever* deserves it most. 67. _____ _____

Name _____ Class _____ Date _____ Score (R ___ × 4) ___

19. GRAMMAR: PRONOUN REFERENCE

(Study G-6.3.)

Write **1** if the boldface word is used **correctly**.
Write **0** if it is used **incorrectly**.

Example: Gulliver agreed with his master that **he** was a Yahoo. 0

1. David won the lottery and quit his job. **This** was unexpected. 1. 0
2. Betsy told Alison that **she** didn't follow through enough. 2. 1
3. Alf decided to drop out of college. He later regretted **that** decision. 3. 0
4. On the white card, list the classes **that** you plan to take this year. 4. 1
5. Tom thought of Nick because **he** owed him a favor. 5. 1
6. In England, **they** call a *bumper* a *fender*. 6. 1
7. I was late filing my report, **which** greatly embarrassed me. 7. 0
8. On her return from Europe, **they** stopped her at Customs. 8. 1
9. She was able to complete college after earning a research assistantship. We greatly admired her for **that**. 9. ___
10. We suggested that the players stage *Falstaff*, but **it** was not well received. 10. ___
11. Reluctantly, the princess used her third wish, **which** canceled the first two thoughtless ones. 11. ___
12. They planned to climb sheer Mount Maguffey, a feat **that** no one had ever accomplished. 12. ___
13. Pat always wanted to be a television newscaster; thus she majored in **it** in college. 13. ___
14. Barkum denounced the use of arbitration in the dispute, **which** was not popular with the workers. 14. ___
15. **It** was well past midnight when the phone rang. 15. ___
16. The speaker kept scratching his head, a mannerism **that** proved distracting. 16. ___
17. **It** says in the paper that the President's popularity is declining. 17. ___
18. When Pete retires, **they** will probably give him a gold watch. 18. ___
19. When Schultz presented his highly negative criticism of the play, the professor said she thought **it** was well written. 19. ___
20. Eric started taking pictures in high school. **This** interest led to a brilliant career in photography. 20. ___
21. **It** will probably not start snowing until Ken reaches home. 21. ___
22–23. In some vacation spots, **they** add the tip to your bill and then give poor service. **This** isn't a way to treat a customer. 22. ___
  23. ___
24–25. In some parts of wartime Europe **it** was so bad that **they** died like flies. 24. ___
  25. ___

32

| Name _____ | Class _____ | Date _____ | Score (R _____ × 5) _____ |

20. GRAMMAR: PHRASES

(Study G-7.)

In the first column, write the number of the **one** set of underlined words that is a **prepositional phrase**.
In the second column, write the number that tells how that phrase is **used** in that sentence:

7. as adjective   8. as adverb

		Phrase	Use
Example: The starting pitcher for the Dodgers is a left-hander.		2	7
1. When we came downstairs; a cab was awaiting us at the curb.	1.	3	8
2. The red-brick building erected in the last century collapsed last week without warning.	2.	4	8
3. After each session the noted professor and his assistant answered the audience's questions.	3.	1	7(8)
4. What they saw before the door closed shocked them beyond belief.	4.	(2)	8
5. No one here has ever seen such consummate grace of style.	5.	4	8(7)
6. The poetry of Wordsworth's early years is what his reputation rests on.	6.	2	
7. This may be what you want, but it's not within my price range. (?2)	7.		
8. A strange call like a crow's can worry us, for it means that enemy scouts are nearby.	8.	4	
9. Since they knew who he was, they held him in spite of the law that forbids any such detention. (?)	9.	1	
10. Through extended negotiations the disputing parties reached an agreement that had long seemed impossible.	10.	1	

If the words in boldface are **a verbal phrase** (infinitive, gerund, or participial), write **1** in the first column and **one** of the following numbers in the second column:

2. verbal phrase used as **adjective**
3. verbal phrase used as **adverb**
4. verbal phrase used as **noun**

If the boldface words are **not a verbal phrase**, write **0** in the first column and nothing in the second column.

		Phrase	Use
Example: *Singing in the rain* is a sure way to get wet.		1	4
Example: Gene is *singing in the rain* despite his cold.		0	
1. *Taking portrait photographs of children* is her means of earning a living.	1.		

33

2. These days she is **taking portrait photographs of children** as her means of earning a living. 2. _____ _____
3. **To work in the theater,** she had to accept a low salary. 3. _____ _____
4. She devoted all her energies **to her work in the theater.** 4. _____ _____
5. Houses **constructed of stone** can last centuries. 5. _____ _____
6. The houses were **constructed of stone** to last centuries. 6. _____ _____
7. His idea of a thrill is **driving in stock-car races.** 7. _____ _____
8. **Driving in stock-car races,** he not only gets his thrills but earns prize money. 8. _____ _____
9. Nowadays he is **driving in stock-car races** for thrills and money. 9. _____ _____
10. He would like **to spend his life as a race driver.** 10. _____ _____

Name _____ Class ____ Date ____ Score (R ____ × 4) ____

21. GRAMMAR: VERBAL PHRASES

(Study G-7.2.)

Classify each boldface verbal phrase:

1. **infinitive phrase** used as noun
2. **infinitive phrase** used as adjective
3. **infinitive phrase** used as adverb
4. **present participial phrase**
5. **past participial phrase**
6. **gerund phrase**

(Use the first column for the first phrase, the second column for the second.)

Example: *Thrilled by her results,* Elaine began *applying to several colleges.*   5   6

1. *Seeing the traffic worsen,* Adam chose *to wait until after rush hour.*   1. 4 3
2. *Obtaining a ticket at that late hour* was not easy *to do.*   2. 6 2
3. *Controlling acid rain* is a crucial step in *protecting our lakes and rivers.*   3. 6 4
4. *Intrigued by what he was saying,* she forgot *to go to her science class.*   4. 5 1
5. *Knowing his potential,* I agreed that John was the man *to select for the position.*   5. 6 3
6. Try *to slip away* without *telling your friends where you are going.*   6. ___ ___
7. I can't help *admiring her;* did you object to *my praising her work?*   7. ___ ___
8. I appreciate *your helping us;* will you be able *to help us again?*   8. ___ ___
9. *Loaded down with library books,* she tried *to open the front door.*   9. ___ ___
10. *Preparing his history assignment* was not as hard *to do* as he had anticipated.   10. ___ ___
11. *Wearing caps and gowns,* the graduates began *to march into the auditorium.*   11. ___ ___
12. Garcia tried *to run the whole mile,* but he was too tired *to do more than a single lap.*   12. ___ ___
13. The speaker, *obviously resenting our interruptions,* frowned at us as we tried *to ask other questions.*   13. ___ ___
14. *Hiking seven miles over mountain trails* is sport *demanding endurance.*   14. ___ ___
15. The students left, *commenting enthusiastically about the speaker* and *hoping to have her return.*   15. ___ ___
16. To try to pass the test without *studying for it* was not a wise thing *to do.*   16. ___ ___
17. *Alarmed by the rapid spread of the measles epidemic,* the health authorities had no alternative but *to vaccinate as many children as possible.*   17. ___ ___
18. *Not having a college major in mind,* he began *to ask about required courses.*   18. ___ ___
19. *Not knowing her way in the strange city,* she stopped *to ask directions.*   19. ___ ___
20. She tried *to obtain the information* without *asking any direct questions.*   20. ___ ___
21. The student *waiting in your office* has two questions *to ask.*   21. ___ ___
22. *Careless camping* has been the cause of too many forests being *reduced to ashes.*   22. ___ ___

35

23. By **looking carefully,** he found an article that was easy **to understand.**   23. _____ _____
24. **Obviously surprised,** she had not known of our plan **to take her with us.**   24. _____ _____
25. Upon **hearing from my parents,** I decided **to go home for the weekend.**   25. _____ _____

Name _____ Class _____ Date _____ Score (R _____ × 10/3) _____

23. GRAMMAR: CLAUSES

(Study G-8.)

Clause has subject & verb

Classify each boldface clause:

1. **independent (main) clause**
2. **adjective clause**
3. **adverb clause**   } **dependent (subordinate) clause**
4. **noun clause**

Example: Do the dishes **when you're finished eating.** ___3___

1. Elizabethan theater companies performed **where they were welcome.** 1. _3_
2. Elizabethan theater companies performed in towns **where they were welcome.** 2. _1_
3. Elizabethan theater companies knew **where they were welcome.** 3. _2_
4. The student **who made the top grade in the history quiz** is my roommate. 4. _2_
5. **Whether I would be able to go to college** depended on whether I could find employment. 5. _4_
6. **After Jud had written a paper for his English class,** he watched television. 6. _1_
7. While I waited for a bus, **I chatted with friends.** 7. _1_
8. The college counseling center offers help to anyone **who needs it.** 8. _2_
9. There is much excitement **whenever election results are announced.** 9. _3_
10. You may use my pen, but **please don't forget to return it to me afterwards.** 10. _1_
11. My adviser suggested **that I enroll in a special science course.** 11. _____
12. My first impression was **that someone had been in my room quite recently.** 12. _____
13. **The actress** who had lost the Oscar **declared through clenched teeth that she was delighted just to have been nominated.** 13. _____
14. He dropped a letter in the mailbox; **then he went into the library.** 14. _____
15. Her reason for moving into the dormitory is **that she wishes to find new friends.** 15. _____
16. Why don't you sit here **until the rest of the class arrives?** 16. _____
17. The real estate mogul, **who is not known for his modesty,** has named yet another parking lot after himself. 17. _____
18. **Although he is fifty-two years old,** he is very youthful in appearance. 18. _____
19. I vividly recall the day **when I won the high school speech tournament.** 19. _____
20. She lived on a ranch **when she was in Montana.** 20. _____
21. **Why don't you wait** until you have all the facts? 21. _____
22. She is a person **whom everyone respects and admires.** 22. _____
23. He thought carefully **in order that he might avoid further errors.** 23. _____
24. I said nothing except **that I had been unavoidably detained.** 24. _____
25. The hotel **where the Senior Ball will be held** has not yet been selected. 25. _____
26. The trophy will be awarded to **whoever wins the contest.** 26. _____

27. The detective walked up the stairs; *he opened the door of the guest room.* 27. _____
28. Is this the book *that you asked us to order for you?* 28. _____
29. Whistling nervously, Ichabod told himself *that there were no such things as ghosts.* 29. _____
30. Will you tell me *what your plans are for the summer months?* 30. _____

| Name _____ | Class _____ | Date _____ | Score (R _____ × 5) _____ |

24. GRAMMAR: CLAUSES

(Study G-8.)

Identify the **dependent** clause in each sentence by writing its first and last words in the first two columns; in the third column, classify it as:

1. noun
2. adjective
3. adverb

		First	Last	Type
Example: The band was dividing the money when the police arrived.		when	arrived	3
1. The children played where there were lots of toys.	1.			
2. The children looked for a room where there were lots of toys.	2.			
3. The children knew where there were lots of toys.	3.			
4. The student who complained about the food was given another helping.	4.			
5. Whether Camille dyes her hair remains a mystery.	5.			
6. After Jonathan had read the morning paper, he threw up his hands in despair.	6.			
7. While I waited for Derwin, I was able to finish my crossword puzzle.	7.			
8. Professor George gave extra help to anyone who asked for it.	8.			
9. There is always a lot of anxiety whenever exams are held.	9.			
10. The coach decided that I was not going to play that year.	10.			
11. Once more, I waited until I had only one night to write my essay.	11.			
12. Dr. Jackson, who prided himself on his fairness, declared Burton the winner.	12.			
13. Although there was no chance of his accepting, I asked David for a date.	13.			
14. I'll never forget Legree's face when I told him to leave.	14.			
15. Luis remarked that he too had trouble with calculus.	15.			
16. It was the only mistake that I had ever seen Henning make.	16.			
17. Nathan explained how his concern about its electrical system kept him from buying the car.	17.			
18. Most of the audience had tears in their eyes when Juliet died.	18.			
19. I told Pat that I would love to meet his sister.	19.			
20. Jill had to leave her office which was being repainted.	20.			

41

Name _____ Class _____ Date _____ Score (R ___ × 4)

25. GRAMMAR: NOUN AND ADJECTIVE CLAUSES

(Study G-8.2.)

Classify each boldface dependent clause:

                Noun Clause   *Adjective Clause*

1. used as **subject**   3. used as **subjective complement**   5. **nonrestrictive (nonessential)**
2. used as **direct object**   4. used as **object of preposition**   6. **restrictive (essential)**

Example: *That she was incompetent* was clear.   1

1. *Who was the better skier* remained unresolved.   1. 1
2. The programmer *who wrote the new computer game* retired at twenty.   2. 5
3. I don't see how anyone could object to *what the speaker said.*   3. 2
4. Leo married Elsa Vidgren, a young woman *whom he had met in high school.*   4. 5
5. *What he wanted us to do for him* seemed utterly impossible.   5. ____
6. Give the four books to *whoever is going to the library.*   6. ____
7. This is a problem *that almost everyone encounters sooner or later.*   7. ____
8. My worst fear is *that I'll be trapped in an elevator and have to listen to the music.*   8. ____
9. Grindley is a person *who seems to thrive on hard work.*   9. ____
10. We visited the area *where gold had first been discovered.*   10. ____
11. Samuel F. B. Morse, *who is famous for his promotion of the telegraph,* was also a successful portrait painter.   11. ____
12. She little realized on setting out *that the journey would take ten years.*   12. ____
13. The long, black limousine, *which had been waiting in front of the building,* sped away suddenly.   13. ____
14. *Whether or not we shall travel by plane* will be determined by the group.   14. ____
15. *What you decide to do now* is critically important.   15. ____
16. The woman *who wrote this letter* shows remarkable perspicacity.   16. ____
17. The jackpot will be won by *whoever holds the lucky number.*   17. ____
18. Naphtha, *which is highly flammable,* is no longer much used for cleaning.   18. ____
19. Plato argued *that artists should be censored.*   19. ____
20. The alarm sounded at a moment *when the students were seated in the gymnasium.*   20. ____
21. We were appalled by *what he had to tell us regarding the episode.*   21. ____
22. *That the war was already lost* could no longer be denied.   22. ____
23. We visited the courthouse *where the Scopes trial had been held.*   23. ____
24. Len enrolled in astronomy, a subject *that had always appealed to him.*   24. ____
25. The truth is *that she had studied the wrong chapter.*   25. ____

26. GRAMMAR: ADVERB CLAUSES

(Study G-8.2B.)

Classify each boldface adverb clause:

1. time (*when, after, until,* etc.)
2. place (*where, wherever*)
3. manner (*as, as if, as though*)
4. cause (*because, since*)
5. purpose (*that, so that,* etc.)
6. condition (*if, unless,* etc.)
7. concession (*although, though*)
8. result (*that*)
9. degree or comparison (*as, than*)

Example: There would be a recount *if I had my way.* — 6

1. *Because I could not stop for Death,* he kindly stopped for me. — 1. 4
2. The candidate was willing to speak *wherever she could find an audience.* — 2. 2
3. Carl ran *as if his life depended on it.* — 3. 3
4. She has always been able to read much faster *than her brother has.* — 4. 9
5. *If I were you,* I would not ask for special consideration at this time. — 5. 6
6. He planned the program *so that he might have time for an occasional bridge game.* — 6. ___
7. Half of the audience left *before the concert was half over.* — 7. ___
8. People are said to be only as old *as they think they are.* — 8. ___
9. He read extensively *in order that he might be well prepared for the test.* — 9. ___
10. *Unless the weather changes,* I won't wear my galoshes. — 10. ___
11. *Although his grades were satisfactory,* he did not qualify for the scholarship. — 11. ___
12. She had worried so much *that she could no longer function effectively.* — 12. ___
13. *Whether or not you are selected,* you will be notified. — 13. ___
14. *Since you say that you will be happier elsewhere,* I will not oppose your leaving. — 14. ___
15. She was so excited *that she had trouble going to sleep that night.* — 15. ___
16. Do not complete the rest of the form *until you have seen your adviser.* — 16. ___
17. *Although he was only 5 feet 5 inches tall,* he was determined to be a basketball star. — 17. ___
18. *Because Einstein had been a poor student,* his parents did not predict a successful career for him. — 18. ___
19. Roberts preferred to go *where no one would recognize him.* — 19. ___
20. *If the litmus paper turns red,* the substance is an acid. — 20. ___
21. Andre hit the ball so far *that it landed on Waveland Avenue.* — 21. ___
22. She usually received better grades *than her brother did.* — 22. ___
23. This is as far *as the elevator goes.* — 23. ___
24. He keeps silent *unless he is certain of his facts,* doesn't he? — 24. ___
25. She smiled *as if she knew something not known to the rest of us.* — 25. ___

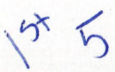

27. GRAMMAR: KINDS OF SENTENCES

(Study G-8.3.)

Classify each sentence:

1. simple   2. compound   3. complex   4. compound-complex

(Any subordinate clauses in the first ten sentences are in boldface.)

Example: He opened the throttle, and the boat sped off.   2

1. Mr. Toad still insisted **that he was an excellent driver.**   1. 3
2. The king, **who was scornful of his advisers,** declared war; he soon regretted his rashness.   2. 4
3. Completion of campus buildings will be delayed **unless funds become available.**   3. 3
4. Consider the matter carefully **before you decide;** your decision will be final.   4. 4
5. This year, either Willis or Kareem will be inducted into the Hall of Fame.   5. 1
6. Geoffrey Chaucer, **who wrote The Canterbury Tales,** died in 1400.   6. 3
7. The storm, **which had caused much damage,** subsided; we continued on our hike.   7. 4
8. We waited **until all the spectators had left the gymnasium.**   8. 3
9. The site for the theater having been selected, construction was begun.   9. 1
10. The skies darkened; the rains came.   10. 2
11. His career as a spy being ended, he settled in Vermont and began his memoirs.   11. 1
12. The beaches are beautiful and uncrowded, and the sun shines most of the time.   12. 2
13. His chief worry was that he might reveal the secret by talking in his sleep.   13. 3
14. Cyrano was sensitive about his long nose; he always imagined that people were making jokes about it.   14. 4
15. The story that appeared in the school paper contained a few inaccuracies.   15. 3
16. The police officer picked up the package and inspected it carefully.   16. 1
17. Because she was eager to get an early start, Sue packed the night before.   17. 3
18. Give the book on ceramics to whoever wants it; we no longer need it.   18. 4
19. Noticing the late arrivals, the speaker motioned them to be seated.   19. 1
20. Who had killed his father was not in doubt; if Hamlet would take his revenge was.   20. 4
21. The suspect went to the police station and turned himself in.   21. 1
22. She is a person who is meticulous about detail.   22. 3
23. Her father, who is an amateur photographer, won a prize in a recent contest.   23. 3
24. Summer, fall, spring—I love any season but winter.   24. 1
25. The house that we wanted had been sold; therefore, we had to look for another one.   25. 4
26. Scientists from all over the world convened to discuss the increasingly serious problem of the greenhouse effect.   26. _____

44

27. Several blockbuster movies were released during the summer, and all were sequels to earlier box-office successes. 27. _____

28. The Chinese government arrested hundreds of persons whom they suspected of pro-democracy sympathies. 28. _____

29. The library contained several boxes of Margaret Mead's field notes which had been made when she worked with the people of New Guinea. 29. _____

30. Although Amy's choreography won praise from the critics, she wasn't satisfied, and she and her company spent the next morning reworking it. 30. _____

31. Did she appear tired? 31. _____

32. The Senate rejected two of the president's cabinet choices but continued to affirm its faith in his leadership. 32. _____

33. Demand for tickets was so strong for the Sniveling Fools concert that the promoters scheduled a second. 33. _____

34. Manuela, who was watching her weight, turned down the double-fudge chewy brownie and instead ordered a bowl of alfalfa bran. 34. _____

35. The Pistons were surprise winners, having defeated the Lakers in four straight games. 35. _____

Name _____ Class _____ Date _____ Score (R ___ × 3, +1) ___

28. GRAMMAR: AGREEMENT—SUBJECT AND VERB

(Study G-9.1.)

Write the number of the **correct** choice.

Example: One of my favorite programs (1)*was* (2)*were* canceled.   1

1. Neither the researcher nor the subject (1)*has* (2)*have* any idea which is the placebo.   1. ___
2. Economics (1)*is* (2)*are* what the students are most interested in.   2. ___
3. Babysitting my cousin's three children (1)*has* (2)*have* exhausted me.   3. ___
4. Not one of the nominees (1)*has* (2)*have* won an Oscar before.   4. ___
5. (1)*Does* (2)*Do* each of the questions count the same number of points?   5. ___
6. The number of college freshmen (1)*has* (2)*have* decreased in recent years.   6. ___
7. Ninety-nine (1)*is* (2)*are* hyphenated because it is a compound number.   7. ___
8. The President, surrounded by a dozen Secret Security agents, (1)*was* (2)*were* to arrive by noon.   8. ___
9. Both the secretary and the treasurer (1)*was* (2)*were* asked to submit reports.   9. ___
10. Everyone in the auditorium (1)*was* (2)*were* startled by the announcement.   10. ___
11. Women (1)*is* (2)*are* a common noun, plural in number.   11. ___
12. Every junior and senior (1)*was* (2)*were* expected to report to the gymnasium.   12. ___
13. There (1)*is* (2)*are* a briefcase, a typewriter, and a tape recorder in the office.   13. ___
14. Ten dollars (1)*is* (2)*are* too much to pay for that book.   14. ___
15. (1)*Is* (2)*Are* there any doughnuts left?   15. ___
16. Neither Margaret nor I (1)*is* (2)*am* (3)*are* going to the fair.   16. ___
17. Each of the suitors (1)*was* (2)*were* sure the princess preferred him.   17. ___
18. (1)*Is* (2)*Are* your father and brother coming to see you graduate tomorrow?   18. ___
19. A typewriter and a sheet of paper (1)*was* (2)*were* all that he needed at the moment.   19. ___
20. There (1)*is* (2)*are* just one chocolate and two vanilla cookies left in my lunch box.   20. ___
21. (1)*Does* (2)*Do* Coach Jasek and the players know about the special award?   21. ___
22. My three weeks' vacation (1)*was* (2)*were* more enjoyable than I had anticipated.   22. ___
23. The only thing that annoyed the speaker (1)*was* (2)*were* the frequent interruptions.   23. ___
24. (1)*Hasn't* (2)*Haven't* either of the officers submitted a written statement?   24. ___
25. The news of his spectacular achievements (1)*comes* (2)*come* as a surprise to all of us.   25. ___
26. On the table (1)*was* (2)*were* a pen, a pad of paper, and two rulers.   26. ___
27. It's remarkable that the entire class (1)*is* (2)*are* passing this semester.   27. ___
28. It (1)*was* (2)*were* your uncle and your cousin who came to see you.   28. ___
29. There (1)*is* (2)*are* many opportunities for part-time employment on campus.   29. ___
30. (1)*Is* (2)*Are* algebra and chemistry required courses?   30. ___

31. One of his three instructors (1)***has*** (2)***have*** offered to write a letter of recommendation.   31. _____

32. (1)***Does*** (2)***Do*** either of your brothers-in-law have jobs?   32. _____

33. Neither I nor my sister (1)***expects*** (2)***expect*** to graduate in June.   33. _____

29. GRAMMAR: AGREEMENT—SUBJECT AND VERB

(Study G-9.1.)

Write the number of the **correct** choice.

Example: Neither Sarah nor her parents (1)*was* (2)*were* ready to leave the fair grounds.   2

1. Virtually every painting and every sculpture Picasso did (1)*is* (2)*are* worth over a million dollars.   1. 1
2. There on the table (1)*was* (2)*were* my wallet and my key chain.   2. 1
3. Neither the documentary about beekeeping nor the two shows about Iceland (1)*was* (2)*were* successful in the ratings.   3. 2
4. Each of the players (1)*hopes* (2)*hope* to make the first team.   4. 2
5. German measles (1)*is* (2)*are* a disease of short duration.   5. 1
6. Sitting on the stairway (1)*was* (2)*were* the instructor and four of her students.   6. 1
7. *Voyages to the Stars* (1)*is* (2)*are* truly exciting reading.   7. 1
8. A political convention, with its candidates, delegates, and reporters, (1)*seems* (2)*seem* like bedlam.   8. 2
9. In the auditorium (1)*was* (2)*were* gathered many students to honor the new officers.   9. 2
10. Each of the visitors (1)*has* (2)*have* been assigned a parking space.   10. 2
11. (1)*Was* (2)*Were* either Rabbi Levine or Father O'Connor asked to speak at the assembly?   11. _____
12. My scissors (1)*was* (2)*were* not where I had left them yesterday.   12. _____
13. His courage, as well as his ability, (1)*makes* (2)*make* him much admired by many.   13. _____
14. High-powered cars (1)*has* (2)*have* become his main interest in life.   14. _____
15. His baseball and his glove (1)*was* (2)*were* all Jamil was permitted to take to the game.   15. _____
16. Neither my friends nor I (1)*expects* (2)*expect* to go on the overnight trip.   16. _____
17. My coach and mentor (1)*is* (2)*are* Mr. Graham.   17. _____
18. Among her most valued possessions (1)*was* (2)*were* a locket and a bracelet.   18. _____
19. The committee (1)*is* (2)*are* unable to come to a decision regarding the scholarship.   19. _____
20. Your carriage, along with its driver and two footmen, (1)*awaits* (2)*await* your every command.   20. _____
21. Where (1)*is* (2)*are* the canoe and the sailboat?   21. _____
22. Corinne, as well as her two cousins, (1)*intends* (2)*intend* to spend the summer here.   22. _____
23. (1)*Has* (2)*Have* either of the books on architecture been returned to the library?   23. _____
24. Neither criticism nor frequent failures (1)*was* (2)*were* enough to retard his progress.   24. _____
25. Where (1)*is* (2)*are* your raincoat and boots?   25. _____
26. The warden, as well as three of the guards, (1)*has* (2)*have* been indicted.   26. _____
27. She is the only one of six candidates who (1)*refuses* (2)*refuse* to speak at the ceremony.   27. _____
28. Neither the officer nor the spectators (1)*was* (2)*were* certain of the robber's identity.   28. _____
29. Economics (1)*has* (2)*have* been the most dismal science I've ever studied.   29. _____
30. (1)*Has* (2)*Have* either of the editorials appeared in the student newspaper?   30. _____

31. It (1)*was* (2)*were* Arnold and Elise who came to see us yesterday while we were away. 31. _____

32. Neither Janet nor her parents (1)*seems* (2)*seem* interested in our offer to help. 32. _____

33. He is one of those fishers who habitually (1)*exaggerates* (2)*exaggerate* the size of the fish caught. 33. _____

Name _____ Class _____ Date _____ Score (R ___ × 3, + 1) ___

30. GRAMMAR: AGREEMENT—PRONOUN AND ANTECEDENT

(Study G-9.2.)

Write the number of the **correct** choice.

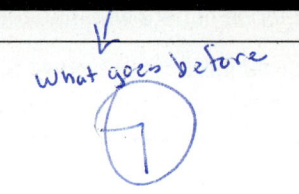

what goes before ⓘ

Example: One of the riders fell off (1)*his* (2)*their* horse.   1

1. Agatha Christie is the kind of writer who loves to keep (1)*her* (2)*their* readers guessing until the last page.   1. 1
2. Vacationers flock to Hawaii because (1)*you* (2)*they* enjoy its awesome scenery and delightful climate.   2. 2
3. If anyone has found my wallet, will (1)*he* (2)*they* please return it.   ✓3. 2
4. He majored in mathematics because (1)*it* (2)*they* had always been of interest to him.   4. 1
5. She presented extensive data, though (1)*it* (2)*they* had been difficult to assemble.   ✓5. 1
6. He assumed that every student had done (1)*his* (2)*their* best to complete the test.   6. 2
7. Both Eddie and Luis decided to stretch (1)*his* (2)*their* legs when the bus reached Albany.   7. 2
8. Neither of the women had ever mentioned (1)*her* (2)*their* difficulties.   ✓8. 2
9. Each of the attorneys spent several hours outlining (1)*his* (2)*their* ideas.   9. 1
10. He buys his books at the campus bookstore because (1)*it has* (2)*they have* low prices.   10. 1
11. Neither the president nor the deans had indicated (1)*her* (2)*their* position.   11. ___
12. Every member of the basketball team received (1)*her* (2)*their* individual trophy.   12. ___
13. Our family made (1)*its* (2)*their* decision to spend less on Christmas this year.   13. ___
14. The jury seemed to be having difficulty in making up (1)*its mind* (2)*their minds.*   14. ___
15. Neither Margaret nor Ellen has paid (1)*her* (2)*their* dues yet.   15. ___
16. Anyone who doesn't turn in (1)*her* (2)*their* uniform will have to pay for it.   16. ___
17. Before someone can choose a career rationally, (1)*he* (2)*they* must have sufficient information.   17. ___
18. Neither the guide nor the hikers seemed aware of (1)*his or her* (2)*their* danger.   18. ___
19. The faculty has already made (1)*its* (2)*their* recommendations.   19. ___
20. I don't know what people see in (1)*those kind* (2)*those kinds* of movies.   20. ___
21. One has to decide early in life what (1)*he* (2)*they* can succeed at.   21. ___
22. Neither the coach nor the players underestimated (1)*his or her* (2)*their* opponents.   22. ___
23. Stan and the stage crew did (1)*his* (2)*their* best to complete the set on time.   23. ___
24. Both the pilot and the copilot thought that (1)*his* (2)*their* hour had come.   24. ___
25. Neither the Mets nor the Cubs (1)*is* (2)*are* likely to win the pennant this year.   25. ___
26. In the London subway, riders pay according to the distance (1)*you* (2)*they* travel.   26. ___
27. If a stranger tried to talk to her, she would just look at (1)*him* (2)*them* and smile.   27. ___
28. Every one of the trees in the affected areas had lost most of (1)*its* (2)*their* leaves.   28. ___

1st 10

32. GRAMMAR: FRAGMENTS

(Study G-10.2A.)

subject verb & stand alone

12 right

Write **1** if the boldface words are a **complete sentence**.
Write **0** if they are a **fragment**.

Example: Luis was famished. *Having eaten only four hot dogs at the game.* — 0

1. The lights flickered and went out. *When the storm struck the coast.* The blackout lasted for hours. — 1. 0
2. *Having applied for dozens of jobs and not having had any offers.* — 2. 0
3. *The manuscript having been returned, Johanna sat down to revise it.* — 3. 1
4. Harrison desperately wanted the part. *Because he believed that this was the film that would make him a star.* — 4. 0
5. *Books, cameras, suitcases, blankets—all of which were piled on the porch.* — 5. 0
6. She was happy. *As a matter of fact, she was delighted.* — 6. 1
7. *The reason for the delay being that we had had a flat tire.* — 7. 0
8. She parked her car. *Then she hurried into the courthouse.* — 8. 1
9. I have the latest news bulletin. *Are you interested in hearing it?* — 9. 0
10. Maurice kept nodding his head as the coach explained the play. *Thinking all the time that it would never work.* — 10. 1
11. *Because she was interested in rocks, she majored in geology.* — 11. 1
12. I argued with two of my fellow students. *First with Edward and then with Henry.* — 12. 0
13. Jackson made some bad investments. *Such as buying desert land and speculating in cocoa beans.* — 13. 1
14. Taylor was absolutely positive he would pass. *Regardless of having received failing grades on both his essay and the midterm.* — 14. 0
15. *Colleen stepped up to the free-throw line; then she made two points to win the game.* — 15. 1
16. *His term paper having been returned.* He looked eagerly for the instructor's grade. — 16. ___
17. *Because he never fully realized how important a college education could be.* — 17. ___
18. She went to the supermarket. *After she had made a list of groceries that she needed.* — 18. ___
19. Two hours before the contest, he was very nervous. *Later, he felt very confident.* — 19. ___
20. I telephoned Dr. Gross. *The man who had been our family physician for many years.* — 20. ___
21. We suspect Atterley of the theft. *Because he had access to the funds and he has been living far beyond his means.* — 21. ___
22. He likes strawberry shortcake. *Especially when it is topped with whipped cream.* — 22. ___
23. Please don't go. *Stay.* — 23. ___
24. She is a star athlete. *Besides being a brilliant student.* — 24. ___
25. I offered her a ticket to *Aïda*. *An opera she had wanted to see.* — 25. ___
26. I planned to spend the summer with Uncle Henry. *My father's youngest brother.* — 26. ___

1st 15

27. ***Knowing that her time was limited, she took a taxi to the station.***   27. _____

28. My leg was in a cast for six months. ***To walk was difficult and painful.*** I became quite depressed.   28. _____

29. I was, however, determined. ***To make my leg as strong as ever.*** Strenuous daily exercises became my regimen.   29. _____

30. Roger Maris never received the credit he deserved. ***Despite breaking Babe Ruth's record for home runs in a single season.***   30. _____

Name _____ Class _____ Date _____ Score (R _____ × 5) _____

33. GRAMMAR: COMMA SPLICES AND FUSED SENTENCES

(Study G-10.2B.)

Write **1** for each item that is a **single complete sentence.**
Write **0** for each item that is a **comma splice** or **fused sentence.**

Example: The mission was a success, everyone was pleased.   0

1. The critics unanimously agreed the play was terrible it closed after a week.   1. 1
2. The party broke up at one in the morning, Ichabod lingered for a few final words with Katrina.   2. 0
3. Fitzgerald's stories paralleled his own life; he wrote often of young men frustrated in love.   3. 0
4. In this story Faulkner deals with the red race, the black race, and the white race alike, his topic is the destruction of the wilderness.   4. 1
5. Determined to sweep the southern and western states, the President authorized extra campaign money to be spent there.   5. 0
6. If the moon enters the earth's shadow, a lunar eclipse occurs, which causes the moon to turn a deep red.   6. 1
7. Say hello to Wendell, if you see him, it's been weeks since he's been here.   7. 0
8. The ticket agent had sold eighty-one tickets to boarding passengers, yet there were only eleven empty seats on the train.   8. 0
9. When I saw what he had done, I couldn't believe my eyes he had repainted the whole room while I was gone.   9. 1
10. The film ended; no one noticed.   10. 0
11. The course was not so difficult as I had thought I earned an A.   11. _____
12. Since she did not believe that humankind's destiny was determined by forces beyond its control, she insisted that people were their own greatest enemies.   12. _____
13. Sheer exhaustion having caught up with me, I had no trouble falling asleep.   13. _____
14. As the music began, Ichabod arose and asked Katrina for a dance.   14. _____
15. The restaurant check almost made me faint, because I had left my wallet home, I couldn't pay for the meal.   15. _____
16. Those of us who owned cars ignored the rule, since we were seniors, we never worried about campus regulations.   16. _____
17. It was a cloudy, sultry afternoon when we sighted our first school of whales, and the cry of "Lower the boats!" rang throughout the ship.   17. _____
18. During the mating dance the female rats would come out of their burrows unexpectedly the males would stop dancing as the population increased.   18. _____
19. Now the war was over; however, nothing really could be done, the refugees could not be reunited with relatives who had come here earlier.   19. _____
20. They didn't try to fix the car, they just abandoned it.   20. _____

Name _____ Class _____ Date _____ Score (R _____ × 3, + 1) _____

34. GRAMMAR: FRAGMENTS, COMMA SPLICES, AND FUSED SENTENCES

(Study G-10.2.)

Write **1** for each item that is a **complete sentence.**
Write **0** for each item that is a **fragment.**

Example: A man who neither seeks out trouble nor avoids it.   0

1. Because pie, ice cream, and candy bars have practically no nutritional value.   1. _____
2. When the bindings release, the ski comes off.   2. _____
3. Which was what the Syrians had wanted in the first place.   3. _____
4. The people Clyde worked with, who all knew him intimately.   4. _____
5. Whereas older cars run on regular gas and lack complex pollution controls.   5. _____
6. This was what the Syrians had wanted in the first place.   6. _____
7. If nothing had come of it, she would have been safe.   7. _____
8. If nothing had come of it, her safety in the workplace being fully assured by an employee benefits contract.   8. _____
9. Which could in no way be rationally explained by any of the scientists.   9. _____
10. Wait.   10. _____

Write **1** for each item that is **one or more complete, correct sentences.**
Write **2** for each item that contains a **fragment.**
Write **3** for each item that contains a **comma splice** or **fused sentence.**

Example: Today is Monday, tomorrow is Tuesday.   3

1. Clyde Griffiths' parents lacked the strength or wisdom to bring up their family properly. Clyde grew ashamed of his parents, his clothes, and his ugly surroundings.   1. _____
2. Clyde grew older, he dreamed of a life of wealth and elegance.   2. _____
3. He spent most of his meager earnings on clothes and luxuries for himself. Contributing little to his parents.   3. _____
4. Clyde managed to impress his wealthy uncle. Who gave him a job at his factory.   4. _____
5. One night Clyde's uncle invited him to a dinner. There he saw wealthy, beautiful Sondra Finchley.   5. _____
6. He became determined to have her, although she was too far above his social position, she lived in elegance.   6. _____
7. Clyde then started going with a factory girl named Roberta; she soon became pregnant by him.   7. _____
8. Sondra, growing to like Clyde, agreed to marry him, this made him see his dreams of wealth and status coming true.   8. _____
9. Meanwhile, Roberta expected Clyde to marry her, and Clyde knew. That if he had to marry her, his dreams would be ruined.   9. _____
10. Remembering a newspaper article about a young woman who had drowned in a rowboat accident, he invited Roberta to go rowing.   10. _____

11. What happened to Clyde, Roberta, and Sondra is told in the novel *An American Tragedy* it was written by Theodore Dreiser.   11. _____

12. He wore a pair of mud-encrusted, flap-soled boots they looked older than he was.   12. _____

13. He wore a pair of mud-encrusted, flap-soled boots, footgear that looked older than he was.   13. _____

14. The computer produced pages of statistics, for the agency wanted to know how its money was spent.   14. _____

15. Enrique reread his assignment a dozen times before handing it in. To be absolutely sure his ideas were clear.   15. _____

16. The representatives decided, however, to wait for the foreign minister's arrival before making a decision.   16. _____

17. That she is dead is beyond dispute.   17. _____

18. "I believe," declared the headmaster. "That you deserve expulsion."   18. _____

19. The scouts hiked two miles until they reached the falls, then they had lunch.   19. _____

20. The police having been warned to expect trouble, every available officer lined the avenue of the march.   20. _____

21. A still greater challenge faced them, it seemed impossible to warn the fort in time.   21. _____

22. Ireland's vital crop had been wiped out by the potato blight, nevertheless, Irish people who owned ten acres of land were disqualified from poor relief.   22. _____

23. The Irish immigrants to the United States did not go into farming for fear that the potato blight would strike there, but the German immigrants did go into farming, they had no fear of this blight.   23. _____

35. GRAMMAR: SENTENCE EFFECTIVENESS

(Study G-10.)

For each **correct** sentence, write **1**.
For each **incorrect** (ineffective) sentence, write the number that **explains** the error:

2. failure to subordinate details
3. childishly choppy sentences
4. overuse of *and*
5. needless separation of subject and verb or parts of infinitive
6. dangling, misplaced, or squinting modifier
7. nonparallel structure
8. omission in comparison or degree
9. shift in person, number, tense, voice, etc.
10. redundancy (including double negative and superfluous *that*)
11. inflated phrasing

Example: He wanted *to shower* and *to sleep.*	1
Example: That was a *most unique* moment.	10
1. If *one* drives a car without thinking, *you* are more than likely to have an accident.	1. 9
2. She said *that,* if I helped her with her math, *that* she would type my paper.	2. 10
3. The entire class was *so* pleased at learning that Dr. Turner had rescheduled the quiz.	3. 8
4. I intended to *carefully and thoughtfully* consider my program for the fall term.	4. 5
5. The director, thinking *only* about how he could get the shot of the exploding car, endangered everyone.	5. 5
6. She *could hardly* hear the speaker because of the noise in the hallway.	6. 1
7. *Looking down from the top of the hill,* the houses appeared to be very small.	7. 6
8. The children learned *to dance* and *singing.*	8. 7
9. She *walks* onto the platform, and then she *began* to speak quietly to the audience.	9. 9
10. He *couldn't hardly* make himself heard because of the noise outside.	10. 10
11. She sat down *and* opened her purse *and* took out her pen *and* began to write.	11. 4
12. He told me *that he was going to write a letter* and *not to disturb him.*	12. 7
13. *Eleanor Gruen is a senior,* and she just won national recognition for her poetry.	13. 2
14. Mike *baked* a cake, and much time *was spent* in frosting it.	14. 9
15. If a *student* knows how to study, *he* should achieve academic success.	15. 1
16. *He went to his office. He sat down. He opened his briefcase. He read some papers.*	16. ___
17. Summer is a time for *parties, friendships, for athletics,* and *in which we can relax.*	17. ___
18. Juliet and I must *make a decision, within one passage of the sun across the heavens, as to whether we should be forever united in holy wedlock.*	18. ___
19. She is *such* a sweet child!	19. ___
20. I shot a bear *in my pajamas.*	20. ___
21. Being a ski jumper requires *nerves of steel, you have to concentrate to the utmost,* and *being perfectly coordinated.*	21. ___

22. **The situation in regard to decisions on the possible expenditure of my monetary resources is such that any commitment on my part to such expenditure must be considered with extreme caution.** 22. _____

23. The plane neither had *enough fuel* nor *proper radar equipment.* 23. _____

24. *My personal opinion is that I think that* the Athletics will win their division by ten games. 24. _____

25. The malfunctioning landing gear *killed nearly* everyone on the plane; only one person survived. 25. _____

Write the number of the **most effective** way of expressing the given ideas.

Example:
1. At this moment in time, I regret that it was impossible for me to partake in my morning repast.
2. I had to skip breakfast.
3. I had not hardly enough time for breakfast.   2

1.
   1. We found a little Hungarian restaurant. It was on Main Street. We went in it to eat.
   2. We went to eat at a little Hungarian restaurant that we found on Main Street.
   3. There was a little Hungarian restaurant on Main Street, and we found it there and went in to eat.   1. 2

2.
   1. The house that my mother bought was located between two gasoline stations.
   2. The house that my mother bought was located where there was a gasoline station on one side of it and another gasoline station on the other side.
   3. The domicile purchased by my maternal parent was juxtaposed to automotive refueling establishments on either side.   2. 1

3.
   1. The terrorists revealed the condition of their hostages well after they demanded food and fuel.
   2. The terrorists wanted food. They wanted the plane refueled. Until then, they didn't reveal the condition of their hostages.
   3. Before revealing the condition of their hostages, the terrorists demanded fuel and food.   3. _____

4.
   1. Harry Truman, who woke up in the morning to find himself elected President, had gone to bed early on election night.
   2. Harry Truman, who had gone to bed early on election night, woke up the next morning to find himself elected President.
   3. Harry Truman went to bed early on election night, and he woke up the next morning and found himself elected President.   4. _____

5.
   1. The papers were marked *top secret*. The term *top secret* indicates contents of extraordinary value.
   2. The papers were of extraordinary value, and therefore they were marked *top secret*.
   3. The papers were marked *top secret,* indicating their extraordinary value.   5. _____

Name _____ Class _____ Date _____ Score (R _____ × 5) _____

36. GRAMMAR: PARALLEL STRUCTURE

(Study G-10.1F.)

11 right

Write **1** if the boldface words or word groups are **all in parallel structure**.
Write **0** if the boldface words or word groups are **not all in parallel structure**.

Example: Lilliputian politicians practiced *leaping* and *creeping*.   1

1. Charlene impressed everyone by her **wit, charm, grace,** and **intelligence.**   1. 1
2. J.R. **put three competitors into bankruptcy, lied to his wife and brother,** and then **his breakfast was brought to him.**   2. 0
3. The apartment could be rented **by the week, by the month,** or **you could pay on a yearly basis.**   3. 1
4. **What I saw, what I did,** and **what I endured** during those tragic days will always haunt my memory.   4. 0
5. Our new wood-burning stove **should keep us warm, save us money,** and **should afford us much pleasure.**   5. 0
6. **Where my father went on Friday nights, what he did there,** and **how much of the family's money he wasted on those occasions,** I never found out until years later.   6. 1
7. Our family Bible is **old, beautiful,** and **has been read by many.**   7. 0
8. The chief ordered agent 007 **to break into the building, crack the safe,** and **to steal the atomic yo-yo plans.**   8. 1
9. Barbara likes especially to **read Tolstoy, sketch landscapes,** and **run in marathons.**   9. 1
10. Losing **his wife to death, his self-control to liquor,** and **the loss of his daughter's custody** brought Charlie to the brink of despair.   10. 0

Write **1** if the sentence **contains parallel structure**.
Write **0** if the sentence **violates parallel structure**.

Example: The candidates took lessons in how to kiss babies and looking honest.   0

1. I knew what I was supposed to do but not when I was supposed to do it or how I could accomplish it.   1. 0
2. The scouts marched briskly off into the woods, trekked ten miles to Alder Lake, and tents were erected by them.   2. 0
3. Rodney, the hero of the novel, had three main characteristics: his ambition, he hated von Stroeblicht, and his love for Maria.   3. 1
4. Carlos liked both painting and operatic singing.   4. 0
5. Carlos liked not only painting but also to sing opera.   5. 1
6. I was born an American, I will live an American, and my death will be as an American.   6. 0
7. The dance committee members realized that they had to either raise the ticket price or find a smaller band.   7. 1
8. Neither regulating prices nor wages will slow inflation enough.   8. 1
9. Tightening the money supply is more effective than if taxes are raised.   9. 1
10. Charlie practiced shooting from the top of the key as well as how to dribble with either hand.   10. 0

60

| Name _____ | Class _____ | Date _____ | Score (R _____ × 10) _____ |

37. GRAMMAR: PARALLEL STRUCTURE

(Study G-10.1F.)

Write **1** if the bold words or word groups are **all in parallel structure**; write **0** if they are not. Then in the last three columns, identify each element as follows:

2. **noun (including gerunds)**
3. **participial**
4. **verb phrase (with or without complement)**
5. **prepositional phrase**
6. **infinitive**
7. **clause**
8. **adjective**

	Parallel	#1	#2	#3
Example: Grandmother insisted on **cleanliness, godliness, and being prompt.**	0	2	2	3

1. Bobby was always **laughing, smiling, and joking.**
2. Hector fought **with great skill, with epic daring, and superb intelligence.**
3. The credo Tennyson's Ulysses cherished was **to strive, to seek, and not yield.**
4. The castle was **built on a hill, surrounded by farmland, and commanded a magnificent view.**
5. Raines can **throw, hit, and he is a good base stealer.**
6. By nightfall, **we were tired, we were hungry, and homesick.**
7. The guerrillas **surrounded the village, set up their mortars, and the shelling began.**
8. Orlando did not know **where she had come from, why she was there, or the time of her departure.**
9. Her favorite pastimes remain **designing clothes, cooking gourmet meals, and practicing the flute.**
10. Eliot's poetry is **witty, complex, and draws on his vast learning.**

38. GRAMMAR: PLACEMENT OF MODIFIERS

(Study G-10.2C, D.)

Write **1** if the boldface word(s) are **correctly** placed.
Write **0** if the boldface word(s) are **incorrectly** placed.

Example: Never give a toy to a child **which can be swallowed.** — 0

1. He ordered a pizza for his friends **covered with pepperoni.** — 0
2. Mr. Andrus spotted a bird sitting on a telephone wire **that he could not identify.** — 1
3. She had enough money to buy **only** two of the three books that she needed. — 0
4. She saw a police officer on a horse, **looking out our fifth-floor window one day.** — 0
5. We knew that to **quickly and thoroughly** cleanse the wound was necessary. — 1
6. We saw the plane taxi onto the field **that would soon be leaving for Chicago.** — 0
7. The Larsons were spending **almost** a third of their income on rent. — 1
8. Derek found a clue in his bedroom **that he had never seen before.** — 1
9. In the basement of the store, we found a sale of **soiled** women's purses. — 1
10. We hurriedly bought a picnic table from a clerk **with collapsible legs.** — 0
11. We learned that no one could discard anything at the municipal dump **except people living in the community.**
12. We had trouble finding a **red, white, and blue** child's violin for the show.
13. Although he has tried several times, he just can't learn to drive a car **with a standard shift.**
14. The bride walked down the aisle with her father **wearing her mother's wedding gown.**
15. Despite his best intentions, he failed to **over the years** return home for Christmas.
16. Naomi's grandfather lived to be **nearly** ninety years old.
17. "This is the best book I **almost** ever read!" she exclaimed.
18. Call, **after you have addressed these 106 envelopes,** me at home.
19. **Only** one teacher seems able to convince Raymond that he should study.
20. She loved the meal prepared for her by her husband **in the microwave.**
21. I had considered **for several days** the possibility of eloping.
22. We watched the QE II as she slowly sailed out to sea **from our hotel window.**
23. Indicate **on the enclosed mimeographed sheet** whether you are going to the class picnic.
24. A **battered** man's hat was hanging on a branch of the tree.
25. He found a pie baked by his wife **on the top shelf of the refrigerator.**
26. She found the wedding dress worn by her mother **hanging in the attic.**
27. He gave the scraps of meat to the dog **that had been left on the dinner plates.**
28. Elmore Hoskins said **when he scored his twenty thousandth point** he would retire.
29. Mary Bell had decided **before her son was two years old** that the boy would be a lawyer.
30. He replied **usually** they went to Paris in the spring.

Name _____ Class _____ Date _____ Score (R _____ × 10/3) _____

39. GRAMMAR: DANGLING MODIFIERS

(Study G-10.2D.)

7 right

Write **1** if the boldface words are used **correctly**.
Write **0** if they are used **incorrectly** (**dangling**).

Example: *Dancing to stardom,* fame is elusive goal. 0

1. *Dreaming of seeing her name in lights,* Wendy bought a bus ticket to New York. 1. 1
2. *Rowing across the lake,* the moon often disappeared behind the clouds. 2. 0
3. *Having walked three miles,* the cabin was a welcome sight to all of us. 3. 1 ✓
4. *While shaving,* the idea for a new play came to him. 4. 1
5. *Trapped alone there at midnight,* the house creaked and moaned with every step. 5. 1 ✓
6. *After roasting for five hours at 325°,* you will have a delicious turkey. 6. 0
7. *Upon entering college,* he applied for part-time employment in the library. 7. 1
8. *When a little girl,* my brother threw a rock at me. 8. 0
9. *To get to Carnegie Hall,* practice must go on for hours every day. 9. 0
10. *To assure a good catch,* the fish should find a fresh, juicy worm on your hook. 10. 0
11. *After waiting for an hour,* word reached us that the speaker had been delayed. 11. _____
12. *When nine years old,* my father took my brother and me on our first camping trip. 12. _____
13. *At the age of ten,* I was permitted to go, for the first time, to a summer camp. 13. _____
14. *After putting away my fishing equipment,* the surface of the lake became choppy. 14. _____
15. *While visiting the zoo,* the chimpanzees entertained the children. 15. _____
16. *To achieve a goal,* a person must expect to work and to make sacrifices. 16. _____
17. *Hanging on a nail in the clothes closet,* my neighbor's plaid jacket had lost its shape. 17. _____
18. *After hearing of Tom's need for financial aid,* a hundred dollars was put at his disposal. 18. _____
19. *To unroll and lay linoleum successfully,* the room must be reasonably warm. 19. _____
20. *Pickled in spiced vinegar,* the host thought the peaches would go with the meat. 20. _____
21. *While reaching for a hammer,* the ladder began to tip. 21. _____
22. *Disappointed at the poor attendance,* the play closed Saturday night. 22. _____
23. *By saving his money for two years,* Arthur was able to finance his trip to Europe. 23. _____
24. *After being cleaned and wrapped in waxed paper,* the fisher put the day's catch in the freezer. 24. _____
25. *Discovering that I had left my wallet at home,* I asked Janet to pay for our lunch. 25. _____
26. *As an infant,* Darlene was up every night at four to feed Teresa. 26. _____
27. *Getting up early,* the house seemed unusually quiet to me. 27. _____
28. Finally, *after working for days,* the garden was free of weeds. 28. _____
29. *To receive a reply to your question,* a self-addressed envelope is needed. 29. _____
30. *After finishing my assignment,* the dog ate it. 30. _____

1st 10

Name		Class		Date		Score (R	× 10)	

40. GRAMMAR: DANGLING MODIFIERS

(Study G-10.2D.)

Write **1** if the boldface words are used correctly.
Write **0** if the boldface words are used incorrectly.
In the second column, write the word to which the boldface words now refer.

Example: *After dancing the lead in* **Swan Lake,** cheers filled the hall.   0   cheers

1. *Writing during the Renaissance,* poems were characterized as speaking pictures.
2. *Approaching New York,* the view of the Manhattan skyline was exciting.
3. *To have a just society,* discrimination in all forms must disappear.
4. *After looking all over the house,* my wallet turned up on my night table.
5. *Before spending a dollar,* Granny always thought twice.
6. *Depressed by his failure to win Daisy,* Gatsby's business ventures suffered.
7. *To get a passing grade in this course,* the professor's little quirks must be considered.
8. *Sleeping until noon each day,* the sunlight shining through the window wouldn't wake me.
9. *While raging against the storm,* King Lear learned of humanity's suffering.
10. *Having read the morning paper,* it was tossed aside.

23. Oh[ ] I had no idea that you would be offended by my frivolous remarks.   23. _____
24. We were asked to read *The Grapes of Wrath*[ ] which is a novel by John Steinbeck.   24. _____
25. Lorraine Hansberry[ ] the author of *A Raisin in the Sun*[ ] died at thirty-five.   25. _____

Name _____ Class _____ Date _____ Score (R ____ × 4) ____

43. PUNCTUATION: THE COMMA

(Study P-1.)

If no comma is needed in the bracketed space(s), write **0** in the blank at the right.
If one or more commas are needed, write in the blank the number (**1** to **10** from the list below) of the **reason** for the comma(s).
(Use only one number in each blank.)

1. parenthetical expression (other than nonrestrictive clause)
2. nonrestrictive clause
3. direct address
4. after *yes* or *no*
5. before *such as, especially,* or *particularly*
6. contrast
7. omission
8. confirmatory question
9. date
10. state or country

Example: The Allies invaded Normandy on June 6[ ] 1944.   9

1. Our house[ ] which had stood since 1901[ ] burned to the ground.   1. 2
2. Senator[ ] would you comment on reports that you will not run again?   2. 3
3. Menlo Park[ ] New Jersey[ ] was Edison's home.   3. 10
4. You would like more pie[ ] wouldn't you?   4. 8
5. You will agree[ ] of course[ ] with the board's decision.   5. 1
6. I hope[ ] Charles and Mary[ ] that you will come to see us often.   6. 3
7. The person[ ] who did that to you[ ] should go to prison.   7. 2(0)
8. For dessert, John ordered strawberry shortcake; Louise[ ] pineapple sherbert.   8. 7
9. Is it true[ ] sir[ ] that you are unwilling to be interviewed by the press?   9. 8(3)
10. Our next contestant comes all the way from Fresno[ ] California[ ] just to be with us today.   10. 10
11. Frank graduated from the University of Michigan; Esther[ ] from Columbia University.   11. 7
12. Students[ ] who work their way through college[ ] learn to value their college training.   12. 0
13. She said, "No[ ] I absolutely refuse to answer your question."   13. ____
14. Fat Albert loves all beautiful things[ ] particularly hamburgers and french fries.   14. ____
15. December 7[ ] 1941[ ] will be remembered as a day of infamy.   15. ____
16. I had wanted to see the janitor[ ] not the apartment-house manager.   16. ____
17. Nevertheless[ ] we were fortunate to have recovered a part of our luggage.   17. ____
18. The instructor told us to read the poem[ ] and to write our impressions of it.   18. ____
19. You are expecting to spend the evening with us[ ] aren't you?   19. ____
20. I've already told you[ ] little boy[ ] that I'm not giving you back your ball.   20. ____
21. Robert Frost[ ] who won the Pulitzer prize for poetry in 1924[ ] was born in San Francisco.   21. ____
22. Not everyone[ ] who objected to the new ruling[ ] signed the petition.   22. ____
23. It was[ ] on the other hand[ ] an opportunity that he could not turn down.   23. ____
24. Dwight Eisenhower[ ] who was our thirty-fourth President[ ] was born on October 14, 1890.   24. ____
25. She has several hobbies[ ] such as collecting coins, writing verse, and growing roses.   25. ____

70

44. PUNCTUATION: THE COMMA

(Study P-1.)

If **no comma** is needed in the bracketed space(s), write **0** in the blank at the right.
If **one or more commas** are needed, write in the blank the number (**1** to **11** from the list below) of the **reason** for the comma(s).
(Use only one number in each blank.)

1. independent clauses joined by *and, but, or, nor, for, yet*
2. introductory adverb clause
3. long introductory prepositional phrase
4. introductory participial phrase
5. introductory infinitive phrase
6. series
7. coordinate adjectives
8. appositive
9. absolute phrase
10. mild interjection
11. direct quotation

Example: James Joyce, Ireland's most famous novelist, lived most of his life abroad. — 8

1. The Dallas Cowboys have good running backs[ ] and look good on defense as well. — 0
2. Well[ ] we'll probably see another foot of snow before the winter ends. — 10
3. Agatha Christie[ ] the famous mystery writer[ ] caricatured herself in her books. — 8
4. Appalled by the restaurant's prices[ ] Katharine vowed never to return. — 4
5. The concert having ended[ ] the fans rushed toward the stage. — 9
6. He hoped to write short stories[ ] publish his poems[ ] and plan a novel. — 6
7. If you wish to go to Italy next spring[ ] I'll plan to go with you. — 2
8. Many people had tried to reach the top of the mountain[ ] but only a few had succeeded. — 1
9. Equipped with only an inexpensive camera[ ] she succeeded in taking a prize-winning picture. — 4
10. During times of emotional distress and heightened tensions[ ] Madeline remains calm. — 3
11. To gather pine cones for Christmas decorations[ ] he traveled far up the mountain. — 5
12. Recognizing that his position was hopeless[ ] Krilov resigned. — 4
13. That it was late[ ] and that we were tired was all too evident. —
14. Mr. Novak found himself surrounded by noisy[ ] exuberant students. — 7
15. "We are[ ]" she said[ ] "prepared to serve meals to a group of considerable size." — 11
16. Jolene had no intention of withdrawing from college[ ] nor was she willing to carry a lighter program. —
17. To master the tuba[ ] one has to practice for years. —
18. Although storm clouds were gathering[ ] we made the trip across the lake in the kayak. —
19. "You must be more quiet[ ] or the landlord will make us move," she said. —
20. We asked Pat Barton[ ] the Explorer Scout director[ ] to suggest a suitable campsite. —
21. I could not decide whether to go to college[ ] or to go to Nigeria with my aunt. —
22. Built on a high cliff[ ] the house afforded a panoramic view of the valley below. —
23. The ringing of the telephone having awakened him[ ] he was unable to go back to sleep. —
24. The professor raised his voice to a shout[ ] the class having apparently dozed off. —
25. Her courses include Russian[ ] organic chemistry[ ] and marine biology. —

45. PUNCTUATION: THE COMMA

(Study P-1.)

In the blank,

    write **1** if the punctuation in brackets is **correct**;
    write **0** if it is **incorrect**.

(Use only one number in each blank.)

Example: We would appreciate it[,] therefore[,] if you paid your bill and left.   1

1. She died[,] because she had been unable to find shelter.   1. 0
2. We traveled to Idaho[,] and went down the Snake River.   2. 1
3. "Tell me," he demanded[,] "who you are."   3. 1
4. When the results were in[,] Marvina was the winner.   4. 1
5. You expect to graduate in June[,] don't you?   5. 1
6. O'Conner started the second half at linebacker[,] O'Hara having torn his knee ligaments.   6. 1
7. O'Conner started the second half at linebacker[,] O'Hara had torn his knee ligaments.   7. 0
8. Trying to concentrate[,] Susan closed the door and turned off the television set.   8. 1
9. "My fellow Kiwanians[,] this is a real opportunity to be of service," he said.   9. 1
10. Some of the older and more conservative members of the tennis club[,] did not approve of Roseanna's dress.   10. 0
11. Judy, who especially enjoys baseball, sat in the front row[,] and watched the game closely.   11. 0
12. "Are you going to a fire?"[,] the police officer asked the speeding motorist.   12. 1
13. Two of the students left the office[,] the third waited to see the dean.   13. _____
14. The coach and three of her players[,] recently appeared on a television program.   14. _____
15. "I won't wait any longer," she said[,] picking up her books from the bench.   15. _____
16. We looked down from our plane on the rugged[,] snow-covered mountains.   16. _____
17. The relatively short drought[,] nonetheless[,] had still caused much damage to the crops.   17. _____
18. The apartment they rented[,] had no screens or storm windows.   18. _____
19. I opened my presents[,] then I cut my birthday cake.   19. _____
20. However[,] much you may think you like ice cream, two quarts will be too much.   20. _____
21. In Berkeley, California[,] on August 18, 1984, Shirley and Don were married.   21. _____
22. "Wait a minute," he said[,] "I have a matter that I wish to discuss with you."   22. _____
23. Her grandfather[,] who has trouble understanding young people today[,] frowned and left the room.   23. _____
24. F. Scott Fitzgerald[,] the author of *The Great Gatsby*[,] grew up in Minnesota.   24. _____
25. Next summer she hopes to fulfill a lifelong wish[,] to travel to Alaska by boat.   25. _____
26. Today let's just sit[,] talk[,] and rest; tomorrow we'll be very busy.   26. _____
27. Her last day in the office[,] was spent in sorting papers and filing manuscripts.   27. _____

28. To enable us to find you in an emergency[,] leave your telephone number at the desk.   28. _____

29. Having booted up her word processor[,] Colleen's quest for the Great American novel began.   29. _____

30. Haven't you any idea[,] of the responsibility involved in running a household?   30. _____

46. PUNCTUATION: THE COMMA

(Study P-1.)

If there should be **a comma** at any one or more of the numbered spaces in a sentence, circle the corresponding number(s) in the column at the right.
If there should be **no commas** in the sentence, circle **0**.

Example: I'll have a hamburger fries and a coke with lots of ice. 0 ① ② 3 4
                1   2   3   4

                                                                                                            0 1 2 3 4

1. Amanda bought paint a roller and two brushes. 1. 0 1 ② ③ 4
2. Because Gulliver believed that all human beings were Yahoos he despised them. 2. 0 1 2 3 ④
3. Phil mixed the eggs onions and peppers before frying them. 3. 0 1 ② ③ 4
4. And now my proud beauty you will do exactly what I say. 4. 0 ① ② 3 4
5. I wanted to go to Harvard; Terry to Yale. 5. 0 1 2 ③
6. No I know nothing regarding her whereabouts. 6. 0 ① 2 3
7. I phoned Jack this morning but he wasn't at home or at work. 7. 0 ① 2 3 4
8. The chairman who had already served two terms in Congress and one in the State Assembly declared his candidacy again. 8. 0 ① 2 ③ 4
9. I was born on December 1 1965 in Fargo North Dakota during a blizzard. 9. 0 ① ② ③ ④
10. I consider him to be a hard-working student but I may be wrong. 10. 0 ① 2 ③ 4
11. Audrey a woman whom I met last summer is here to see me. 11. 0 ① 2 ③ 4
12. Having an interest in anthropology she frequently audited Dr. Irwin's class that met on Saturdays. 12. 0 1 ② 3 ④
13. Her friends her relatives and her husband urged her to reconsider her decision to leave. 13. 0 ① ② ③ 4
14. Well I dislike her intensely but she is quite clever to be sure. 14. 0 ① ② 3 ④
15. To solve her legal problems she consulted an attorney that she knew from college. 15. 0 ① 2 3
16. "To what " he asked "do you attribute your great popularity with the students?" 16. 0 ① ② 3 4
17. Some of the specimens that you will see on display today were alive more than 100,000 years ago when the dinosaurs were masters of the earth. 17. ⓪ 1 2 3 4
18. *Heartbreak House* a comedy by George Bernard Shaw was revived on Broadway in the early 1980s. 18. 0 ① 2 ③ 4

? 19. Richard Cory appeared to all the townspeople to be a successful man; he was nonetheless in
                    1   2   3   4
     profound despair.   19. 0 1̸ 2 3̸ 4̸

20. "You haven't seen my glasses have you?" Granny asked the twins thinking they had hidden them
                                 1   2   3   4
    in her tomato soup.   20. 0 ① 2 ③ 4

21. The car having broken down because of a dirty carburetor we missed the first act in which Hamlet
                            1   2   3   4
    confronts his father's ghost.   21. 0 1̸ ② 3 4

22. After she had paid her tuition she went to the room in the dormitory that she had chosen where
                     1   2   3
    she soon began unpacking her clothes.   22. 0 ① ② ③ 4
          4

23. The day was so warm and sunny that the entire class wished fervently that the lecture would take
                    1   2   3
    place outdoors.   23. 0 1 ② ③̸ 4
         4

24. Linda Ronstadt who has recorded dozens of hit songs has also starred in the operetta *The Pirates*
                  1   2   3   4
    of Penzance.   24. 0 ① ② 3 4

25. The road to Brattleboro being coated with ice we proceeded slowly and cautiously.   25. 0 1̸ ② 3 4
                        1   2   3 4

All

47. PUNCTUATION: THE COMMA

(Study P-1.)

The following sentences have commas that are either incorrect or absent. In the first column, write the word **after** which the comma that is there is wrong OR **after** which a comma is missing.
In the second column, select a reason for making your correction from the list below.
The sentence needs a comma because there is (are):

1. **two independent clauses joined by** and, but, or, nor, for, yet
2. **an introductory adverb clause**
3. **an introductory phrase (long prepositional, participial, infinitive, or absolute)**
4. **a series**
5. **an appositive**
6. **a nonrestrictive clause or phrase**

The comma that is there now is wrong because:

7. **There is no full clause after the conjunction.**
8. **The comma separates the subject from its verb.**
9. **The comma separates the verb from its complement.**
10. **There is a restrictive (or essential) clause.**

	Word	Reason
Example: When Frank and Joe looked around the stranger had vanished.	around	2
Example: The sun, shone brightly.	sun	8

1. There was much to do before her guests arrived for dinner but Betty did not know where to begin.
2. That it is indeed time for extremely serious commitment and concerted action on your part, is evident.
3. Having examined and reexamined the ancient manuscript the committee of scholars declared it genuine.
4. If Professor Fusty can convince the board that she is right, the curriculum will include Chaucer's major poems, and Shakespeare's major tragedies.
5. Michael has ambitious plans to finish his novel, start a play and work on his dissertation.
6. My brother who wants to be a pharmacist, attends Columbia.
7. The character who is wearing the black hat and black cape, is the villain of the piece.
8. The bus having left an hour before we had no choice but to walk.
9. George and Robert thoroughly and painstakingly considered, what had to be done to defuse the bomb.
10. If ever there were the law on one side, and simple justice on the other, here is such a situation.
11. John Irving, the author of *The World According to Garp* has published a new novel.

12. Agatha began with the assumption that Max could not possibly have murdered Commodore Jenkins but she quickly came to doubt his innocence when she saw the footprints under the stairs. 12. _____ ___

13. Claiming that he was just offering good advice Ace frequently would tell me which card to play. 13. _____ ___

14. What gave Barbara the inspiration for her short story, was her mother's account of growing up on a farm. 14. _____ ___

15. Owen's baseball cards included such famous examples as Willie Mays' running catch in the 1954 World Series, and Hank Aaron's record-breaking home run. 15. _____ ___

16. The volume that was the most valuable in the library's rare book collection, was a First Folio edition of Shakespeare's plays. 16. _____ ___

17. A film enjoyed by millions of people throughout the world *Gone with the Wind* was first thought unlikely to be a commercial success. 17. _____ ___

18. With a triumphant cry and a finger pointing directly at Moriarty, Holmes demonstrated once again, that he was unequalled among the world's detectives. 18. _____ ___

19. Nick was disturbed when he learned how Gatsby had made his fortune, but remained convinced of Gatsby's greatness. 19. _____ ___

20. The criminal mind Jessica thought to herself, is even craftier than I had imagined. 20. _____ ___

| Name _____ | Class _____ | Date _____ | Score (R _____ × 4) _____ |

48. PUNCTUATION: THE PERIOD, QUESTION MARK, AND EXCLAMATION POINT

(Study P-2 through P-4.)

Write **1** if the punctuation is **correct**.
Write **0** if it is **incorrect**.
(Use only one number in each blank.)

Example: Are we having fun yet[?] 1

1. You'd like that, wouldn't you[?] 1. 1
2. "Fire in number two engine!" the copilot shouted[!] 2. 0
3. The police officer calmly inquired if I had the slightest notion of just how fast I was backing up[?] 3. 0
4. Mr. Hall and Miss[.] James will chair the committee. 4. 0
5. I can't see you because I have to study all night for a math[.] quiz. 5. 0
6. Chickens, two goats, a pig, etc.[.], were wandering around the farmer's yard. 6. 0
7. Good afternoon, ma'am[.] May I present you with a free scrub brush? 7. 1
8. The homemaker asked[?], "May I know first, young man, what you're trying to sell?" 8. 0
9. His next question—wouldn't you know[?]—was, "What do you need, ma'am?" 9. 0
10. She said, "Is it too much to ask again, 'What are you selling?'[?]" 10. 0
11. "What a magnificent view you have of the mountains[!]" said he. 11. _____
12. Who said, "If at first you don't succeed, [. . .] try again"? 12. _____
13. The man on the street corner told me that the special sale price of the watch would be $25[.] for just another ten minutes. 13. _____
14. HELP WANTED: Executive sec'y[.] with min. 4 yrs. exper. 14. _____
15. Pat, please type this memo[.] to the purchasing department. 15. _____
16. What? You lent that scoundrel Snively $10,000[?!] 16. _____
17. I asked her why, of all the men on campus, she had chosen him[?] 17. _____
18. Why did I do it? Because I loved her[.] Renée was the finest person I've ever known. 18. _____
19. Footloose and Fancy Free[.] [title of an essay] 19. _____
20. Would you please send me your reply by return mail[.] 20. _____
21. Your son ate my goldfish[?] Why didn't you just make him a hamburger? 21. _____
22. Charlie was an inspiring[(?)] date. He had me yawning all evening. 22. _____
23. "I can't [. . .] remember [. . .] her name," Sir Reginald gasped as the poison took effect. 23. _____
24. You must bring the following: (1[.]) your bat, (2[.]) your glove, and (3[.]) your baseball shoes. 24. _____
25. I heard the news on station W[.]I[.]N[.]K. 25. _____

78

Name _____ Class _____ Date _____ Score (R ___ × 5) ___

49. PUNCTUATION: THE SEMICOLON

(Study P-5.)

Using the following list, write the number of the **reason** for the semicolon in each sentence. (Use only one number in each blank.)

1. between independent clauses *not* joined by any conjunction or conjunctive adverb
2. between independent clauses joined by a conjunctive adverb (*however, therefore,* etc.)
3. between clauses joined by *and, but, or, nor, for,* or *yet* but having internal commas
4. to group items in a series

Example: Everyone predicts the Mets will win the World Series; let's just wait and see.   *1*

1. Congress has now voted to spend more to protect wildlife; however, it may be already too late for many species.   1. 2
2. The farmers are using an improved fertilizer; thus their crop yields have increased.   2. 2
3. Still to come were Perry, a trained squirrel; Armand, an acrobat; and Marlene, a magician.   3. 4
4. "Negotiations," he said, "have collapsed; we will strike at noon."   4. 1
5. Read the questions carefully; answer each one as briefly as possible.   5. 1
6. Don first attended Houghton; then he went to the University of Michigan.   6. 1 ②
7. Pam, who lives in the suburbs, drives her car to work each day; yet Ruben, her next-door neighbor, takes the bus.   7. 3
8. She had paid her dues; therefore, she was eligible to vote.   8. 2
9. We stopped in Laramie, Wyoming; Omaha, Nebraska; and Des Moines, Iowa.   9. 4
10. Cora was a fatalist; she believed that all events are predetermined.   10. 1

If **a semicolon** is needed within the brackets, insert it; then in the blank at the right, write the number (**1** to **4** from the list above) of the **reason** for that semicolon.
If **no semicolon** is needed within the brackets, write **0** in the blank.
(Use only one number in each blank.)

Example: I couldn't help you with your assignment[;] moreover, I wouldn't.   *2*

1. She is going to the concert on Friday[;] do you want her to get tickets for us?   1. 1
2. Shall I telephone to find out the time[ ] when the box office opens?   2. 0
3. Many of my college friends live in dormitories[;] some still live at home.   3. 1
4. Louise read the Help Wanted ads[ ] and went to the Campus Employment office for weeks until, to her great relief, she found a summer job.   4. 0
5. She is very gifted[;] two of her poems appear in an anthology.   5. 1
6. The surprises in Rodger's starting lineup were Garcia, the second baseman[;] Hudler, the shortstop[;] and Fitzgerald, the catcher.   6. 4
7. I was late for work[ ] because I had trouble finding a parking space.   7. 0
8. The subway was packed with commuters[;] we were obliged to stand.   8. 1
9. Her boarding house burned down[;] consequently, she had to find new lodgings.   9. 2
10. I tried several times to learn typing[;] but, unfortunately, never succeeded.   10. 3 ⓪

79

Name _____ Class _____ Date _____ Score (R _____ × 10/3) _____

50. PUNCTUATION: THE SEMICOLON AND THE COMMA

(Study P-1 and P-5.)

Within the brackets, insert a comma, a semicolon, or nothing—whichever is **correct**. Then, in the blank at the right,
  write **1** if you inserted **a comma** within the brackets;
  write **2** if you inserted **a semicolon**;
  write **0** if you inserted **nothing**.
(Use only one number in each blank.)

Example: The referee dropped the puck[;] the game began. _2_

1. The river remained calm[ ] still the guide refused to take us across. 1. _2_
2. Tony signed the petition to maintain the green space downtown[ ] but several of his friends argued that the city needed investment. 2. _1_
3. Dr. Jones[ ] who teaches geology[ ] graduated from MIT. 3. _0_ _0_
4. The Dr. Jones[,] who teaches geology[,] graduated from MIT. 4. _1_ _0_
5. I met the woman[ ] who is to be president of the new junior college. 5. _1_ _0_
6. She likes working in Washington, D.C.[ ] she hopes to remain there permanently. 6. _2_
7. For the teenagers, the program was entertaining[ ] for the adults, it was boring. 7. _2_
8. Read the article carefully[ ] then write an essay on the author's handling of the subject. 8. _1_ _2_
9. I shall have to borrow a magazine[ ] because I left my copy at home. 9. _1_ _0_
10. The game being beyond our reach[ ] the coach told me to start warming up. 10. _2_ _1_
11. We are going on a cruise around the bay on Sunday[ ] and we'd like you to come with us. 11. _____
12. If Amy decides to become a lawyer[ ] you can be sure she'll be a good one. 12. _____
13. I had worked in the library before[ ] therefore, I had no trouble getting a part-time job. 13. _____
14. Li-Young registered for an advanced biology course[ ] otherwise, she might not have been admitted to medical school. 14. _____
15. I would like[ ] however[ ] to pay the bridge toll for you. May I? 15. _____
16. The new rug has been delivered[ ] however, Terry is not pleased with its color. 16. _____
17. He began his speech again[ ] fire engines having drowned out his opening remarks. 17. _____
18. She somehow manages to find friends[ ] wherever she goes. 18. _____
19. Let me introduce the new officers: Phillip Whitaker, president[ ] Elaine Donatelli, secretary[ ] and Pierre Northrup, treasurer. 19. _____
20. The car did not need a new starter[ ] it needed only a tune-up. 20. _____
21. We had known the Floyd Archers[ ] ever since they moved here from New Jersey. 21. _____
22. During the summer we visited friends in Chicago[ ] New York[ ] and Toronto. 22. _____
23. The drama coach was a serene person[ ] not one to be worried by nervous amateurs. 23. _____
24. To turn them into professional performers was[ ] needless to say[ ] an impossible task. 24. _____
25. "No matter how hard I work," Frank said[ ] "I never seem to get an A." 25. _____

26. Call the security office[ ] if there seems to be any problem with the locks.   26. _____

27. She moved to California[ ] after she had sold her farm in North Dakota.   27. _____

28. Britain was the first Common Market country to react[ ] others quickly followed suit.   28. _____

29. The tanker ran aground in perfectly fair weather and calm seas[ ] the captain was fired.   29. _____

30. Because the weather was bad[ ] the picnic was moved indoors.   30. _____

Name _____ Class _____ Date _____ Score (R _____ × 1%) _____

51. PUNCTUATION: THE SEMICOLON AND THE COMMA

(Study P-1 and P-5.)

Within the brackets, insert a comma, a semicolon, or nothing—whichever is **correct.** Then, in the blank at the right,

write **1** if you inserted **a comma** within the brackets;
write **2** if you inserted **a semicolon;**
write **0** if you inserted **nothing.**

(Use only one number in each blank.)

Example: The television blared[;] the children sat motionless.   2

1. Felicia's father launched into his usual diatribe about the younger generation[ ] the room quickly emptied. 1. 1 (2)
2. Into the cauldron the witches put a newt's eye[ ] a frog's toe[ ] and a pinch of henbane. 2. 1
3. "You're wondering why I called you here, aren't you?"[ ] the leader asked. 3. 0
4. The lead runner crested the hill[ ] and glanced back at the others struggling far behind. 4. 1
5. The score was tied[ ] the game would go into overtime. 5. 2
6. Blenchford studied all night[ ] but failed the test. 6. 1 (0)
7. Do you know[ ] Ms. Lane[ ] how we can get in touch with Superman? 7. 1
8. The first building on campus was an old[ ] dilapidated[ ] three-story structure. 8. 1
9. Time having run out[ ] I was obliged to hand in my test paper before I had finished. 9. 1
10. I spend too much time watching late shows on television[ ] I should be studying instead. 10. 2
11. All farmers[ ] who have had their crops destroyed by this year's drought[ ] will be compensated. 11. _____
12. Having written down the wrong page number[ ] I read the wrong chapter. 12. _____
13. She had been in the hospital[ ] she had missed three weeks of classes. 13. _____
14. During his first three years of college[ ] he attended three different institutions. 14. _____
15. Having learned that the meeting had been postponed[ ] John went back to the library. 15. _____
16. Poised and completely at ease[ ] the student-body president greeted the incoming freshmen. 16. _____
17. "The answer is here somewhere," Holmes said[ ] "and I'm sure we can find it." 17. _____
18. We stood shivering[ ] the sun having gone behind the clouds. 18. _____
19. Ms. Vane, the principal, waited[ ] until the students in the assembly hall were quiet. 19. _____
20. The mayor adjusted his tie, smiled, and coughed[ ] then he said he was glad that the question had been asked. 20. _____
21. Having my arm in a cast bothered me[ ] but the doctor insisted that a cast was necessary. 21. _____
22. In a nearby park, children were shouting happily[ ] their noise did not disturb us. 22. _____
23. Professor Curtis has left the campus[ ] however, she may be reached by telephone. 23. _____
24. This certainly is the best of all possible worlds[ ] don't you think? 24. _____
25. They were married[ ] while they were still seniors in college. 25. _____

26. After they graduated, they packed their belongings[ ] and moved to a small town in Ohio.　26. _____
27. Amy was aware as she raced down the hill[ ] that this would be her last chance ever to win a medal in the downhill.　27. _____
28. He teaches freshman English[ ] Speech II[ ] and a literature course.　28. _____
29. Your behavior is unacceptable, Mr. Flashman[ ] we shall have to expel you.　29. _____
30. Our representatives included Will Leeds, a member of the Rotary Club[ ] Augusta Allcott, a banker[ ] and Bill Rogers, president of the Chamber of Commerce.　30. _____
31. The President ordered his aides to start an inquiry into the oil spill[ ] and to report back to him within the week.　31. _____
32. She expects to graduate in June[ ] then she will spend the summer in Europe.　32. _____
33. He followed the trail to the summit[ ] later, he found the entrance to the mine.　33. _____
34. "She is," the coach said, "an excellent golfer[ ] and a fine student."　34. _____
35. Without seeing where I made my mistakes on my essay[ ] I simply can't hope to do better next time.　35. _____
36. Peter lives in Minnesota[ ] Howard, in New York.　36. _____
37. The teacher asked[ ] that everyone be quiet.　37. _____
38. His adviser's signature being required[ ] Fred went to the administration building.　38. _____
39. Failing to make the right turn on the highway[ ] caused us to arrive two hours late.　39. _____
40. Fighting his way through a host of tacklers[ ] he scored a touchdown.　40. _____
41. My uncle's barn[ ] not his house[ ] had burned to the ground.　41. _____
42. As Mark Twain said, the rain will stop[ ] it usually does.　42. _____
43. Upon graduating from college[ ] he went into the service.　43. _____
44. Vacation time is almost over[ ] there are only four days left.　44. _____
45. "When we go to Canada[ ] I would like to stay for a week in Victoria," she said.　45. _____
46. After attending his chemistry and psychology classes[ ] Leslie sat down to write a letter.　46. _____
47. We didn't go to the theater[ ] for we had heard that no good seats were left.　47. _____
48. Frank was angry with Gail[ ] for having broken her promise to him to be prompt.　48. _____
49. He asked you to help him with his biology[ ] didn't he?　49. _____
50. They suspected it might be found[ ] if someone were to look through the gym lockers.　50. _____
51. We decided not to watch the late television show[ ] all of us wanting to get a good night's sleep.　51. _____
52. The World Series hadn't yet begun[ ] however, he had equipped himself with a new transistor radio.　52. _____
53. I couldn't remember having seen her as radiantly happy[ ] as she now was.　53. _____
54. No, I cannot go to the game[ ] I have a term paper to finish.　54. _____
55. "I don't know the answer[ ] in fact, I didn't hear your question," she said indifferently.　55. _____
56. Victor[ ] on the other hand[ ] played the best game of his career.　56. _____
57. Genevieve laughed hysterically[ ] Eunice, on the other hand, was very serious.　57. _____
58. "There will be no rain today[ ]" she insisted. "The weather forecaster says so."　58. _____
59. The stores were crowded[ ] the Christmas rush having started.　59. _____
60. Although he majored in math in college[ ] he has trouble dividing a lunch check.　60. _____

52. PUNCTUATION: THE APOSTROPHE

(Study P-6.)

Woman's belongs to women; women's' belongs to more than 1

In the first column, write the number of the **correct** choice (**1** or **2**).
In the second column, write the number (**3** to **6**, from the list below) of the **reason** for your choice. (If your choice has **no apostrophe,** write nothing in the second column.)

3. singular possessive   5. contraction
4. plural possessive   6. plural of letter, number, symbol, word used as word

	Word Choice	Reason for Choice
Example: The day is (1)our's (2)ours.	2	4
1. I (1)*didn't* (2)*did'nt* have enough money with me to pay the taxi.	1. 1	5
2. The (1)*Smith's* (2)*Smiths* have invited us to their daughter's wedding.	2. 2̶ (2)	✗
3. The (1)*James'* (2)*Jameses* are moving to Seattle.	3.	✗
4. My (1)*brother-in-law's* (2)*brother's-in-law* wife is a pediatrician.	4. 1	3
5. The (1)*Russo's* (2)*Russos* have a two-year-old son.	5. 2	
6. Our family cat was delighted with (1)*its* (2)*it's* very own scratching post.	6. 1	
7. The principal demanded, "(1)*Who's* (2)*Whose* responsible for this vandalism?"	7. 1	5
8. The two (1)*girl's* (2)*girls'* talent was quite evident to everyone.	8. 2	4
9. We will be at the (1)*Lopez's* (2)*Lopezes'* home until midnight.	9. 2	4
10. It will be a two-(1)*day's* (2)*days'* drive to the ocean.	10. ✗2	✗4
11. He went on a three (1)*weeks'* (2)*week's* vacation trip to Puerto Rico.	11.	
12. To get ahead, she planned to win her (1)*bosses* (2)*boss's* favor.	12.	
13. After the long absence, they fell into (1)*each others'* (2)*each other's* arms.	13.	
14. From its friendly greeting, it was evident that the dog was (1)*her's* (2)*hers.*	14.	
15. Geraldine uses too many (1)*ands* (2)*and's* in most of her speeches.	15.	
16. His (1)*O's* (2)*Os* have a solid black center; his typewriter needs to be cleaned.	16.	
17. (1)*Wer'ent* (2)*Weren't* you surprised to see him so soon?	17.	
18. Is this Dan and Betty's canoe, or is it (1)*ours* (2)*our's*?	18.	
19. Georgiana insisted, "I (1)*have'nt* (2)*haven't* seen Sandy for weeks."	19.	
20. He bought fifty (1)*cents* (2)*cents'* worth of popcorn.	20.	
21. The back alley was known to be a (1)*thieve's* (2)*thieves'* hangout.	21.	
22. There were far too many (1)*but's* (2)*buts* in his praise of my essay.	22.	
23. He noticed that the (1)*children's* (2)*childrens'* shoes were caked with mud.	23.	
24. "Your (1)*times* (2)*time's* up," announced the testing officer.	24.	
25. The (1)*coal miner's* (2)*coal miners'* union went on strike for higher wages.	25.	

53. PUNCTUATION: THE APOSTROPHE

(Study P-6.)

For each bracketed apostrophe,

write **1** if it is **correct;**
write **0** if it is **incorrect.**

(Use the first column for the first apostrophe in each sentence; use the second column for the second apostrophe.)

Example: *Who*[']*s* on first? Where's *todays*['] lineup?	1	0
1. This is no one *else*[']*s* fault but *your*[']*s*, I'm sorry to say.	1. 1	0
2. Mrs. *Jackson*[']*s* invitation to the *William*[']*s* must have gone astray.	2. 1	0
3. He *would*[']*nt* know that after only two *day*[']*s* employment.	3. 0	0
4. *Wer*[']*en't* they fortunate that the damaged car wasn't *their*[']*s*?	4. 0	0
5. *It*[']*s* a pity that the one bad cabin would be *their*[']*s*.	5. 1	0
6. *We*[']*re* expecting the *Wagner*[']*s* to meet us in Rome next summer.	6. 1	0
7. "*Where*[']*s* your driver's license?" was the *officer*[']*s* first question.	7.	
8. "What Mary *does*[']*nt* know *won*[']*t* worry her," he said.	8.	
9. The two sisters had agreed that *they*[']*d* not wear each *others*['] clothes.	9.	
10. *She*[']*s* the sort of person who won't listen to *anybody*[']*s* opinion but her own.	10.	
11. The *childrens*['] balloons were distributed at my little *sister*[']*s* birthday party yesterday afternoon.	11.	
12. *He*[']*s* hoping to get two *hours*['] work each day in the school cafeteria.	12.	
13. The idea of starting a scholarship fund was not *our*[']*s;* it was *Lois*[']*s*.	13.	
14. There are three *i*[']*s* in the word *optimistic;* there are two *r*[']*s* in the word *embarrass*.	14.	
15. The computer printout consisted of a series of *1*[']*s* and *0*[']*s*.	15.	
16. I sent two dozen red *roses*['] to the members of the *Mothers*['] Club.	16.	
17. I really *did*[']*nt* expect to see all of the *drivers*['] finish the race.	17.	
18. Is it possible that you *hav*[']*ent* heard about the fire at the *Jone*[']*s* house?	18.	
19. Tabby, usually the *mices*['] tormentor, *was*[']*nt* interested in chasing them any longer.	19.	
20. I'm sure that, if *he*[']*s* physically able, *he*[']*ll* play in next Saturday's football game.	20.	
21. The responsibility for notifying club members is *her*[']*s*, not *our*[']*s*.	21.	
22. *Can*[']*t* I persuade you that *you*[']*re* now financially able to own your own car?	22.	
23. I sent word to the *Cohens*['] that *we*[']*d* see them on Sunday.	23.	
24. The address on the envelope was not *our*[']*s;* it was the *Burgesses*['].	24.	
25. My *mother-in-law*[']*s* books are aimed at the *children*[']*s* market.	25.	

85

Name _____ Class _____ Date _____ Score (R _____ × 3, + 1) _____

54. PUNCTUATION: THE APOSTROPHE

(Study P-6.)

In the paragraph below, every word ending in *s* has a number beneath it. Only **eleven** of these words need apostrophes. In each corresponding blank at the right,

write **1** if the word should end in **'s**;
write **2** if the word should end in **s'**;
write **0** if the word needs **no apostrophe.**

Example: We took showers after the game.
                        40   0

A high school athletes fondest dreams concern athletic scholarships to colleges. If a schools
               1   2   3   4   5
basketball star averages twenty points a game or makes an all-star team, that youngsters phone rings
         6   7   8   9   10
constantly, and his or her mail carriers bag overflows with offers from colleges. Yet very often this
              11   12   13   14   15   16
young players hopes are falsely aroused by offers of financial aid that turn out to be no better than
     17   18   19
a nonathletes aid. Recruiters descriptions of tree-shaded campuses overflowing with lively, eager
  20   21   22   23
members of the opposite sex can stimulate a city youths imagination to the point where no reality can
  24   25
match what the minds eye envisions. This young persons disappointment becomes all the keener
        26   27   28   29
when he or she learns that the aid offers from all those colleges are too low for the dreams fulfillment.
             30   31   32   33

1. 2 1
2. 0
3. 0
4. 0
5. 1
6. 0
7. 0
8. 0
9. 1
10. 0
11. 0

12. 1
13. 0
14. 0
15. 0
16. 0
17. 1
18. 0
19. 0
✓20. 2 ①
21. 2
22. 0
23. 0
24. 0
25. 2 ①
✓26. 0 ①
27. 0
28. 1
29. 0
30. 0
31. 0
32. 0
✓33. 0 (1or2)

All 33

55. PUNCTUATION: ITALICS

(Study P-7.)

Write the number of the **reason** for each use of italics:

1. title of book, magazine, or newspaper
2. title of musical production, play, film, or TV show
3. name of ship, aircraft, or spacecraft
4. title of painting or sculpture
5. foreign word not yet Anglicized
6. word, letter, figure, or symbol referred to as such
7. emphasis

Example: I read nothing but *TV Guide*.   1

1. The *Titanic* was thought to be an unsinkable ship. — 1. 3
2. *The Wizard of Oz* seems to be shown on television every Easter. — 2. 2
3. For many years the Manchester *Guardian* has been a leading newspaper in England. — 3. 1
4. Much comment resulted from a recent article in *Harper's* magazine. — 4. 1
5. Directions on the test indicated that all questions were to be answered with *1*'s or *2*'s. — 5. 6
6. A mnemonic device for helping a student to spell the word *principal* is the expression "The *principal* is your *pal*." — 6. 7
7. Susan learned to spell the word *villain* by thinking of a *villa in* Italy. — 7. 7
8. She subscribes to *Time*, *Ms.*, and *Newsweek* magazines. — 8. 1
9. Shakespeare's *Hamlet* is to be the next production of the Little Theater group. — 9. 2
10. An article had been written recently about the submarine *Nautilus*. — 10. 3
11. Tom Wolfe's book about the space program is called *The Right Stuff*. — 11. 1
12. How many *s*'s and *i*'s are there in *Mississippi*? — 12. 6
13. Many American sports lovers consider *Sports Illustrated* one of their favorite magazines. — 13.
14. The American pronunciation of *vase* is *vās*; the British pronunciation is *väz*. — 14.
15. Russell Baker of the *New York Times* has won Pulitzer prizes for commentary and biography. — 15.
16. "Even though you are very busy, you *must* get more rest," said the doctor. — 16.
17. Aboard the *Enterprise*, the captain made plans to return to the planet Zircon to rescue Mr. Spock. — 17.
18. He has a leading role in the opera *Pagliacci*, hasn't he? — 18.
19. She went to Italy aboard the luxury liner *Michelangelo*. — 19.
20. The first American to orbit the earth was John Glenn in *Friendship 7*. — 20.
21. Her printed *R*'s and *B*'s closely resemble each other. — 21.
22. Although he never held office, Lopez was the *de facto* ruler of his country. — 22.
23. Some people spell and pronounce the words *athlete* and *athletics* as if there were an *e* after the *th* in each word. — 23.
24. Dustin Hoffman's portrayal of an autistic savant in *The Rain Man* won him his second Oscar. — 24.
25. The original meaning of the word *mad* was "disordered in mind" or "insane." — 25.

In each sentence there is **one** word or set of words that should be **italicized.** Underline these words, and write in the blank the number (**1** to **7,** from the list on page 88) of the **reason** for the italics.

Example: We were all on the cover of <u>Newsweek.</u>   1

1. "Home Thoughts from Little Moose" is a poem in Ogden Nash's collection <u>The Face Is Familiar.</u>   1. ____
2. Deciding to come home by ship, we made reservations on the <u>Queen Elizabeth II.</u>   2. ____
3. Geraldine went downtown to buy copies of <u>Esquire, Time,</u> and <u>Field and Stream.</u>   3. ____
4. "I shall return" said MacArthur, and he <u>did.</u>   4. ____
5. <u>Brighton Beach Memoirs</u> was a prize-winning play in 1983.   5. ____
6. The <u>New York Times</u> must have weighed ten pounds last Sunday.   6. ____
7. <u>The Body Human</u> was a highly praised television documentary of the early 1980s.   7. ____
8. Bellow's <u>Herzog</u> has always been one of Edward's favorite books.   8. ____
9. Among the magazines lying on the table was a copy of <u>Harper's.</u>   9. ____
10. <u>Fences,</u> August Wilson's play about fathers and sons, won both the Tony and the Pulitzer.   10. ____
11. When I try to pronounce the word <u>statistics,</u> I always stumble over it.   11. ____
12. She seems unaware of the difference between the words <u>accept</u> and <u>except.</u>   12. ____
13. "There is no such word as <u>alright,</u>" said Miss Williams, frowning as she wrote it on the chalkboard.   13. ____
14. Picasso's <u>Guernica</u> depicts the horrors of war.   14. ____
15. <u>The Thinker</u> is a statue that many people admire.   15. ____
16. <u>Lawrence of Arabia</u> is considered an outstanding motion picture of the 1960s.   16. ____
17. You'll enjoy reading "The Man of the House" in the book <u>Fifty Great Short Stories.</u>   17. ____
18. The British spelling of the word <u>humor</u> is h-u-m-o-u-r.   18. ____
19. "What Is College For?" is an essay by Max McConn in <u>Modern English Readings.</u>   19. ____
20. Michelangelo's <u>Last Judgment</u> shows "the omnipotence of his artistic ability."   20. ____
21. The source of the above quotation is the <u>Encyclopaedia Britannica.</u>   21. ____
22. The fourth opera in this winter's series is Verdi's <u>Don Carlo.</u>   22. ____
23. Her argument was <u>ad hominem.</u>   23. ____
24. Perry won the spelling bee's award for creative expression with his rendition of <u>antidisestablishmentarianism.</u>   24. ____
25. The instructor said that Sam's <u>7's</u> and his 4's look very much alike.   25. ____

Name _____ Class _____ Date _____ Score (R _____ × 4) _____

56. PUNCTUATION: QUOTATION MARKS

(Study P-8.)

Insert **quotation marks** (double or single, as needed) at the proper places in each sentence. Then, in the blank at the right, write the number (**1** to **12** from the list below) of the **reason** for the quotation marks:

1. direct quotation
2. title of chapter
3. title of magazine article
4. title of short story
5. title of essay
6. title of poem
7. title of song
8. title of one-act play
9. title of lecture
10. title of newspaper article or editorial
11. definition
12. nickname

Example: *Expedite* means to facilitate or advance.   11

1. The article about silk, The Queen of Textiles, appeared in *National Geographic* magazine in January 1984.   1. 3
2. Murder in the Rain Forest, which appeared in *Vanity Fair* magazine, told of the death of a courageous Brazilian environmentalist.   2. 3
3. W. C. Fields' dying words were I'd rather be in Philadelphia.   3. 1
4. The poem The Swing was written by Robert Louis Stevenson.   4. 6
5. I am confident, said the candidate, that I will win.   5. 1
6. Use of the Dictionary is a chapter in the textbook *Correct Writing*.   6. 2
7. In the magazine *Arizona Highways,* Joyce Muench, in an article titled In the Kingdom of the Skies, describes the unusual cloud formations that enhance Arizona scenery.   7. 3
8. The word *cavalier* was originally defined as a man on a horse.   8. 11
9. Gordon Red Johnson stood up to address the members of the football team.   9. 12
10. Silent Night is a song heard frequently during the Christmas season.   10. 7
11. One of my favorite short stories is Eudora Welty's A Worn Path.   11. 4
12. Did the professor give the lecture Abnormal Behavior last semester?   12. 9
13. The World Is Too Much with Us is a poem by William Wordsworth.   13. 6
14. The Younger Generation is an article that appeared in *Time* magazine.   14. 3
15. An article that appeared in the *Washington Post* is Can We Abolish Poverty?   15. 10
16. Bacon's essay, Of Fortune, comments sadly on the brevity of human friendship.   16. _____
17. The Love Song of J. Alfred Prufrock is a poem by T. S. Eliot.   17. _____
18. The Moon of the Caribbees is a one-act play by Eugene O'Neill.   18. _____
19. The concluding song of the evening was Auld Lang Syne.   19. _____
20. We read a poem by Edna St. Vincent Millay entitled Love Is Not All.   20. _____
21. Civic Responsibility is the title of an editorial in the Denver *Post*.   21. _____
22. Otis took hitting lessons from Harry The Hat Walker.   22. _____
23. We read Marriage Is Belonging, an essay by Katherine Porter.   23. _____

24. She enjoyed Arthur Foff's short story, Beautiful Golden-Haired Mamie. 24. _____

25. *Discography* means a comprehensive list of recordings made by a particular performer or of a particular composer's work. 25. _____

57. PUNCTUATION: QUOTATION MARKS

(Study P-8.)

Write **1** if the punctuation in brackets is **correct**.
Write **0** if it is **incorrect**.
(Use only one number in each blank.)

Example: "Want to play ball, Scarecrow[?]" the Wicked Witch wondered, a ball of fire in her hand. 1. 1

1. The late arrivals asked[, "]When did the party end?" 1. 1
2. When the job was finished, the worker asked, "How do you like it[?"] 2. 1
3. In the first semester, we read Joyce's "The Dead[".] 3. 1
4. "Where are you presently employed?[",] the interviewer asked. 4. 0
5. "Whenever I see Joan," said Ellen[, "]she always asks for you." 5. 1
6. Who was it who mused "Where are the snows of yesteryear["?] 6. 0
7. Dr. Nelson, my math teacher, asked, "Who wants me to repeat the explanation[?"] 7. 1
8. "You're out of your mind![",] exclaimed Lydia, slamming down her books. 8. 0
9. "Write when you can[,"] Mother said as I left for the airport. 9. 1
10. *To sympathize* means ["]to share in suffering or grief[."] 10. 1
11. "Ask not what your country can do for you[;"] ask what you can do for your country." 11. ___
12. The bus driver said, "To the east is the courthouse.["] ["]Buses stop there every half hour." 12. ___
13. "Do you remember Father's saying, 'Never give up[''?"] she asked. 13. ___
14. She began reciting the opening lines of Elizabeth Barrett Browning's sonnet: "How do I love thee? Let me count the ways[."] 14. ___
15. Gwendolyn Brooks's poem ["]The Bean Eaters["] is one of her best. 15. ___
16. ["]The Fantastiks["] is the longest-running musical play in American theater. 16. ___
17. She said, "Don't you get tired of hearing everyone sing 'Mother Machree[?' "] 17. ___
18. "Shall I read aloud Whitman's poem, 'Out of the Cradle Endlessly Rocking[?"] she asked. 18. ___
19. Have you read Adrienne Rich's poem "Necessities of Life[?"] 19. ___
20. When she saw his new Corvette, she exclaimed, "What a beautiful car[!"] 20. ___
21. The noun *neurotic* is defined as "an emotionally unstable individual[".] 21. ___
22. "I'm going to the newsstand," he said[; "]for a copy of the *Atlantic*." 22. ___
23. "Do you believe in fairies[?"] Peter Pan asks the children. 23. ___
24. How maddening of her to reply calmly, "You're so right["!] 24. ___
25. "Come as soon as you can," said Mother to the plumber[. "]The basement is already flooded." 25. ___
26. I heard Andy say, "Hank asked, 'Who are the new neighbors down the street[?']" 26. ___
27. "The Lottery[,"] a short story by Shirley Jackson, was discussed in Janet's English class. 27. ___
28. Did you read Krutch's article, "Is the Common Man Too Common?["?] 28. ___

29. "Was the treaty signed in 1815[?"] the professor asked, "or in 1814?"   29. _____
30. The mayor said, "I guarantee that urban renewal will move forward rapidly[;"] however, I don't believe him.   30. _____

58. PUNCTUATION: ITALICS AND QUOTATION MARKS

(Study P-7 and P-8.)

Write the number of the **correct** choice.

Example: A revival of Cole Porter's play (1)*Anything Goes* (2)"Anything Goes" is playing at the Beaumont Theatre.   __1__

1. (1)"Cats," (2)*Cats,* which is one of Broadway's most successful plays, is based on the work of T. S. Eliot.   1. __2__
2. An editorial titled (1)*Public Transit Needs Public Money* (2)"Public Transit Needs Public Money" appeared in the *New York Times.*   2. __2__
3. (1)"London Bridge" (2)*London Bridge* is a popular nursery rhyme.   3. __1__
4. Paul Kennedy's book (1)*The Rise and Fall of the Great Powers* (2)"The Rise and Fall of the Great Powers" discusses how nations become politically and militarily dominant.   4. __1__
5. The title of the *Harper's* article is (1)*Faculty Survival* (2)"Faculty Survival."   5. __2__
6. The closing song around the campfire was (1)"Good Night, Ladies." (2)*Good Night, Ladies.*   6. __1__
7. (1)*A Haunted House* (2)"A Haunted House" is a short story by Virginia Woolf.   7. __2__
8. The brevity of Carl Sandburg's poem (1)*Fog* (2)"Fog" appealed to her.   8. __2__
9. Helene received (1)*A's* (2)"A's" in three of her classes this fall.   9. __1__
10. She used too many (1)*and's* (2)"and's" in her introductory speech.   10. __1__
11. (1)*Science and Religion* (2)"Science and Religion" is an essay by Albert Einstein.   11. _____
12. He has purchased tickets for the opera (1)"Faust." (2)*Faust.*   12. _____
13. A careless printer had misspelled the word (1)*psychology.* (2)"psychology."   13. _____
14. Dr. Baylor spent two classes on Wallace Stevens' poem (1)"The Idea of Order at Key West." (2)*The Idea of Order at Key West.*   14. _____
15. His favorite newspaper has always been the (1)*Times.* (2)"Times."   15. _____
16. (1)"Our Town" (2)*Our Town* is a play by Thornton Wilder.   16. _____
17. The word *altogether* means (1)"wholly" or "thoroughly." (2)*wholly* or *thoroughly.*   17. _____
18. (1)*What Women Want* (2)"What Women Want" is an essay by Margaret Mead.   18. _____
19. James Thurber's short story, (1)*The Secret Life of Walter Mitty,* (2)"The Secret Life of Walter Mitty," amused her.   19. _____
20. The Players' Guild will produce Marlowe's (1)*Dr. Faustus* (2)"Dr. Faustus" next month.   20. _____
21. Herbert Kim's essay (1)*The Design of a PASCAL Compiler* (2)"The Design of a PASCAL Compiler" appeared in the May 1987 edition of *The Journal of Computer Languages.*   21. _____
22. (1)*Perspectives* (2)"Perspectives" is the title of the textbook we were to use.   22. _____
23. I purchased a copy of Robert Frost's (1)"Collected Poems." (2)*Collected Poems.*   23. _____
24. Our film class saw Truffaut's (1)*Shoot the Piano Player* (2)"Shoot the Piano Player" last week.   24. _____
25. She read (1)*Dover Beach,* (2)"Dover Beach," a poem by Matthew Arnold.   25. _____

26. (1)*Pygmalion* (2)"Pygmalion" is a play by George Bernard Shaw. 26. _____
27. You fail to distinguish between the words (1)*range* and *vary*. (2)"range" and "vary." 27. _____
28. I read a poem by Yeats titled (1)"The Cat and the Moon." (2)*The Cat and the Moon.* 28. _____
29. She rarely purchases copies of (1)*Reader's Digest.* (2)"Reader's Digest." 29. _____
30. (1)*Bound East for Cardiff* (2)"Bound East for Cardiff" is a one-act play by O'Neill. 30. _____

Name _____ Class _____ Date _____ Score (R ____ × ½ + 8) ____

59. PUNCTUATION: THE COLON, THE DASH, PARENTHESES, AND BRACKETS

(Study P-9 through P-12.)

The Colon

Write **1** if the colon in brackets is used **correctly**.
Write **0** if it is used **incorrectly**.

Example: We invited: Larry, Moe, and Curly.   0

1. Casey's first question was[:] Can anybody here play this game?   1. __1__
2. The coach signaled the strategy[:] we would try a double steal on the next pitch.   2. __0__
3. Dear Sir[:] My six years' experience as a legal secretary qualifies me for the position advertised. 3. __1__
4. Dear "Stretch"[:] The whole group—all eight of us—plan to spend the weekend with you.   4. __0__
5. Lara's shopping list included these items: truffles, caviar, champagne, and a dozen hot dogs. 5. __1__
6. The carpenter brought his[:] saw, hammer, square, measuring tape, and nails.   6. __0__
7. Children usually enjoy[:] candy, ice cream, and cookies.   7. ____
8. She began her letter to Tom with these words[:] "You are a stupid fool!"   8. ____
9. I knew that her plane left on Tuesday at approximately 3[:]30 P.M.   9. ____
10. The dean demanded that[:] the coaches, the players, and the training staff meet with him immediately. 10. ____
11. Tonight's winning numbers are[:] 169, 534, and 086.   11. ____
12. She was warned that the project would require one thing[:] perseverance.   12. ____

The Dash, Parentheses, and Brackets

Set off the boldface words by inserting the **correct** punctuation. Then write the number of the punctuation you inserted:

1. dash(es)   2. parentheses   3. brackets

Example: Senator Aiken **Rep. Maine** voted for the proposal.   2

1. It's raining too hard to go to school today *just look out the window.*   1. __1__
2. Holmes had deduced *who knew how?* that the man had been born on a moving train during the rainy season. [*Punctuate to indicate a sharp interruption.*] 2. __1__
3. He will be considered for *this is between you and me, of course* one of the three vice-presidencies in the firm. [*Punctuate to indicate merely incidental comment.*] 3. __2__
4. I simply told her *and I'm glad I did!* that I would never set foot in her house again. [*Punctuate to indicate merely incidental comment.*] 4. __2__
5. Within the last year, I have received three *or was it four?* letters from her. [*Punctuate to indicate merely incidental comment.*] 5. __2__

96

6. At Yosemite National Park we watched the feeding of the bears *from a safe distance, you can be sure.* [*Punctuate to achieve a dramatic effect.*]   6. __1__
7. Her essay was entitled "The American Medical System and It's *sic* Problems."   7. __3__
8. The rules for using parentheses *see page 7* are not difficult to master.   8. __2__
9. Only one thing stood in the way of his buying the yellow Cadillac *money.*   9. _____
10. The statement read: "Enclosed you will find one hundred dollars *$100* to cover damages."   10. _____
11. ELECTRA *with a cry:* Oh! You liar!   11. _____
12. *Eat, drink, and be merry* gosh, I can hardly wait for study week.   12. _____
13. The essay begins: "For more than a hundred years *from 1337 until 1453* the British and French fought a pointless war." [*Punctuate to show that the boldface expression is inserted editorially.*]   13. _____
14. The concert begins at *by the way, when does the concert begin?*   14. _____
15. Getting to work at eight o'clock every morning *I don't have to remind you how much I dislike getting up early* seemed almost more than I cared to undertake. [*Punctuate to indicate merely incidental comment.*]   15. _____
16. She said, "Two of my friends *one has really serious emotional problems* need psychiatric help." [*Punctuate to achieve a dramatic effect.*]   16. _____
17. Campbell's work on Juvenal *see Reference* is an excellent place to start.   17. _____
18. Julius was born in 1900 *?* and came west as a young boy.   18. _____
19. Gerri had only one aim in life *to follow in her mother's footsteps in the medical profession.*   19. _____
20. I'll play *what can I play?*   20. _____
21. Churchill told a cheering House of Commons, "You *Hitler* do your worst, and we will do our best." [*Punctuate to show that the boldface expression is inserted editorially.*]   21. _____
22. I would never consider selling my grandmother's earrings *unless you increase your offer.*   22. _____
23. This should be the third out *oh no, the ball bounces off Smith's helmet!*   23. _____
24. BATMAN *in a shocked tone:* He's taken my what?   24. _____
25. To start the program, simply *1* insert the disk in drive A, and *2* turn on the power switch.   25. _____

Name _____ Class _____ Date _____ Score (R ____ × 10/3) _____

60. PUNCTUATION: THE HYPHEN

(Study P-13.)

Write **1** if the use or omission of a hyphen is **correct**.
Write **0** if it is **incorrect**.

Example: *Seventy six* trombones led the big parade. 0

1. Mr. Pollard's major research interest was **seventeenth-century** French history. 1. ___
2. Dana made a **semi-serious** effort to pick up the check. 2. ___
3. Debbie certainly is a good, old-fashioned, **all-American** girl. 3. ___
4. "I **c-c-can't** breathe," the child panted. 4. ___
5. The **six-year-old** boy climbed onto the speaker's platform and sat down. 5. ___
6. She rented a **two room** apartment on the other side of town. 6. ___
7. The speaker was **well known** to everyone connected with administration. 7. ___
8. A **well-known** scientist will conduct a seminar during summer session. 8. ___
9. The team averaged over **fifty-thousand** spectators a game. 9. ___
10. The contractor expects to build many **five-** and **six-room** houses this year. 10. ___
11. The club president sent a **skillfully-worded** statement to the city editor. 11. ___
12. We sent Joanne a new **five dollar** bill for her birthday. 12. ___
13. I sent in my subscription to a new **bi-monthly** magazine. 13. ___
14. **Semi-infinite** space, the television producer explained, is where the captain and crew will find the semifinal frontier. 14. ___
15. Susan had found her **mother-in-law** to be a very helpful person with the children. 15. ___
16. At last her dream of an **up to date** kitchen was coming true. 16. ___
17. He made every effort to **recover** the missing gems. 17. ___
18. She had bought fabric with which to **re-cover** her husband's favorite chair. 18. ___
19. Yossarian had another long chat with **excorporal** Wintergreen. 19. ___
20. At **eighty-two,** Aunt Mary is as active as ever. 20. ___
21. Charles will run in the **hundred yard** dash next Saturday. 21. ___
22. "The children are not to have any more **c-a-n-d-y,**" said Mother. 22. ___
23. After he graduated from college, he became manager of the **student-owned** bookstore. 23. ___
24. The idea of a **forty hour** week appealed to the workers. 24. ___
25. A world record had been set in the **120 yard** high hurdles. 25. ___
26. Baird played **semi-professional** baseball before going into the major leagues. 26. ___
27. Customers began avoiding the **hot-tempered** clerk in the shoe department. 27. ___
28. His friends tried to restore Al's **self-confidence.** 28. ___
29. Congratulations, Myrtle—you've won a sensational, fantastic, **brand new** gum irrigator! 29. ___
30. Myrtle's gum irrigator was **brand new.** 30. ___

98

Name _____ Class _____ Date _____ Score (R _____ × 1⅔%) _____

62. PUNCTUATION: REVIEW

(Study P.)

Write **1** if the punctuation in brackets is **correct**.
Write **0** if it is **incorrect**.
(Use only one number in each blank.)

Example: The church bells[,] have been ringing all morning.   0

1. He found math difficult[;] but, because he worked so hard, he earned a *B*.   1. 1
2. The Messicks were late[,] their car battery having gone dead.   2. 1
3. I wondered what Shirley was doing[?]   3. 0
4. Dear Dr. Stanley[;] Thank you for your letter of May 10.   4. 0
5. Rafael enjoyed inviting his friends[,] and preparing elaborate meals for them; however, most of his attempts were disasters.   5. 0
6. When the clerk brought out the red coat, Vera asked, "How much is it["?]   6. 0
7. I remembered Dad's remark: "I promised not to say, [']I told you so![']"   7. 1
8. "You may use my car," she said[,] "I won't be needing it today."   8. 1
9. A novella by Conrad, a short story by Lawrence, and some poems of Yeats[,] were all assigned for the last week of the semester.   9. 1
10. She arrived in Baton Rouge, Louisiana[,] last Saturday.   10. 1
11. The children's enthusiasm about going to the zoo was greater than our[']s.   11. ____
12. The relief workers specifically requested food, blankets, and childrens['] clothing. 12. ____
13. He opened his briefcase[,] he took out his notes and began to talk.   13. ____
14. Whenever he speaks, he's inclined to use too many *and-uh*[']s between sentences.   14. ____
15. Someone should tell his wife[;] the only person who can help him overcome this fault. 15. ____
16. The last employee to leave the office is responsible for the following[,] turning off all machines, extinguishing all lights, and locking all executives' office doors.   16. ____
17. Everwhere there were crowds shouting anti[-]American slogans.   17. ____
18. This is the game all America[']s been waiting for—the Super Bowl.   18. ____
19. During the whole wretched ordeal of his trial[;] Charles Darnay remained outwardly calm. 19. ____
20. More than twenty minutes were cut from the original version of the film[,] the producers told neither the director nor the writer.   20. ____
21. December 3, 1966[,] is the date of my birth.   21. ____
22. The fugitive was located near Butte, Montana[,] in a deserted farmhouse.   22. ____
23. The temperature sinking fast as dusk approached[,] we decided to seek shelter for the night. 23. ____
24. MacArthur's forces landed at Inchon[;] thus cutting off the North Koreans.   24. ____
25. My only cousin[,] who is in the U.S. Air Force[,] is stationed in the Arctic.   25. ____
26. Any U.S. Air Force officer[,] who is stationed in the Arctic[,] receives extra pay.   26. ____

101

27. Good grief! Did she agree to that[?!]   27. _____
28. Heidi did not break the record in the marathon[,] she missed it by two-tenths of a second.   28. _____
29. Murphy's boss commended him on his frankness and spunk; then he fired Murphy.   29. _____
30. He wanted[,] to tell the truth[,] but lacked the courage.   30. _____

63. MECHANICS: CAPITALS

(Study M-2.)

Write **1** if the boldface words are **correct** in use or omission of capital letters.
Write **0** if they are **incorrect**.

Example: Cajuns speak a dialect of **french.**   0

1. They met at the **North Side Jewish Center.**   1. _____
2. My brother teaches **high school.**   2. _____
3. The **turkish** bath is closed.   3. _____
4. Mario's uncle is a Catholic **Priest.**   4. _____
5. When will **Congress** convene?   5. _____
6. He is a **Senior** at Harvard.   6. _____
7. My daughter graduated from **Stanford University.**   7. _____
8. He always disliked **Algebra.**   8. _____
9. Mars is the **god** of war.   9. _____
10. I greeted **Professor** Allen.   10. _____
11. She met three **Professors** today.   11. _____
12. "Do you live here?" **she** asked.   12. _____
13. I love the colors of **Fall.**   13. _____
14. The deaths were reported in **the Times.**   14. _____
15. I was born in the **Midwest.**   15. _____
16. Her **Aunt Miriam** has returned.   16. _____
17. He's late for his **economics** class.   17. _____
18. Jane was **President** of her class.   18. _____
19. Woods was promoted to **Major.**   19. _____
20. My **Grandfather** wrote to me.   20. _____
21. I enrolled in **english** and art.   21. _____
22. He began his letter with "My **Dear** Mrs. Johnson."   22. _____
23. He ended it with "Yours **Truly.**"   23. _____
24. We once lived in the **South.**   24. _____
25. I passed German but failed **Calculus.**   25. _____
26. He entered **College** last fall.   26. _____
27. My **father** is an executive.   27. _____
28. I asked **Father** what he meant.   28. _____
29. He goes to **Taft High School.**   29. _____
30. Has the **senate** elected a majority leader yet?   30. _____
31. The twins are now **Seniors.**   31. _____
32. The chess champion is from the **Junior Class.**   32. _____
33. Emma is a **junior** in high school.   33. _____
34. I spent the summer with my **Cousin.**   34. _____
35. Her favorite subject is **french.**   35. _____
36. The tourists visited the **Grand Canyon.**   36. _____
37. I went **East** to a convention.   37. _____
38. He enrolled in **Physics 2.**   38. _____
39. This is a **Baptist Church.**   39. _____
40. I saw Sid (**What** is his last name?) downstairs.   40. _____
41. This is **NOT** my idea of fun.   41. _____
42. A box of **chinaware** was damaged.   42. _____
43. She earned a **Ph.D.** degree.   43. _____
44. The **World Series** had ended.   44. _____
45. She declared that charity is considered a **Christian** virtue.   45. _____
46. His father fought in the Vietnam **war.**   46. _____
47. The chairperson of the **Department of Computer Sciences** is Dr. MacIntosh.   47. _____
48. He said simply, "**my** name is Bond."   48. _____
49. **"Champion of the World"** is a chapter from a book by Maya Angelou.   49. _____
50. She spent her **Thanksgiving** vacation in Iowa with her cousins.   50. _____

Name _____ Class _____ Date _____ Score (R _____ × 5) _____

64. MECHANICS: CAPITALS

(Study M-2.)

In the first column, write the number of the **first correct** choice (**1** or **2**).
In the second column, write the number of the **second correct** choice (**3** or **4**).

Example: Wandering (1)*West* (2)*west*, Max met (3)*Milly* (4)*milly*.   __2__   __3__

1. Macy's Department (1)*Store* (2)*store* is having a great sale on Italian (3)*Shoes.* (4)*shoes.*   1. _____ _____
2. Her (1)*Father* (2)*father* went (3)*South* (4)*south* on business.   2. _____ _____
3. The new (1)*College* (2)*college* is seeking a (3)*President* (4)*president.*   3. _____ _____
4. I was told to begin my letter with "My (1)*Dear* (2)*dear* (3)*Sir* (4)*sir.*"   4. _____ _____
5. I ended it with "Very (1)*Truly* (2)*truly* (3)*Yours* (4)*yours.*"   5. _____ _____
6. After (1)*Church* (2)*church* we walked across the Brooklyn (3)*Bridge* (4)*bridge.*   6. _____ _____
7. The (1)*Headwaiter* (2)*headwaiter* bowed deferentially to his (3)*Royal* (4)*royal* guests.   7. _____ _____
8. The young (1)*Lieutenant* (2)*lieutenant* prayed to the (3)*Lord* (4)*lord* for courage in the coming battle.   8. _____ _____
9. My (1)*Sister* (2)*sister* now lives in the (3)*South* (4)*south.*   9. _____ _____
10. The (1)*President* (2)*president* addresses (3)*Congress* (4)*congress* tomorrow.   10. _____ _____
11. Edna Barney, (1)*M.D.* (2)*m.d.,* once taught (3)*Biology 4* (4)*biology 4.*   11. _____ _____
12. Dr. Galloway, (1)*Professor* (2)*professor* of (3)*English* (4)*english* is now on leave.   12. _____ _____
13. She always does well in (1)*French* (2)*french* and (3)*Math* (4)*math* courses.   13. _____ _____
14. "I'm also a graduate of Scripps (1)*College,*" (2)*college,*" (3)*She* (4)*she* added.   14. _____ _____
15. The pastor of St. Paul's Episcopal (1)*Church* (2)*church* is an (3)*Australian.* (4)*australian.*   15. _____ _____
16. Vera disagreed with the review of (1)*The* (2)*the* Heidi Chronicles in (3)*The* (4)*the* New York Times.   16. _____ _____
17. The club (1)*Secretary* (2)*secretary* said that the minutes of the meeting were "(3)*Almost* (4)*almost* complete."   17. _____ _____
18. The (1)*Girl Scout* (2)*girl scout* leader pointed out the (3)*Milky Way* (4)*milky way* to her troop.   18. _____ _____
19. She read Language (1)*In* (2)*in* Thought (3)*And* (4)*and* Action.   19. _____ _____
20. Her office is in (1)*Room* (2)*room* 218 of Hartley (3)*Hall.* (4)*hall.*   20. _____ _____

Name _____ Class _____ Date _____ Score (R _____ × 3, + 1) _____

65. MECHANICS: NUMBERS AND ABBREVIATIONS

(Study M-4 and M-5.)

Write the number of the **correct** choice.

Example: That book is (1)**3** (2)**three** days overdue.   __2__

1. (1)**1968** (2)**The year 1968** will be remembered as a turbulent time in the United States.   1. _____
2. Several states have raised the drinking age to (1)**twenty-one.** (2)**21.**   2. _____
3. (1)**Prof.** (2)**Professor** Hilton teaches Oriental philosophy.   3. _____
4. Lincoln was born in (1)**Ky.** (2)**Kentucky.**   4. _____
5. Why is there no (1)**thirteenth** (2)**13th** floor in this building?   5. _____
6. The contest will be held at noon on (1)**Fri.** (2)**Friday.**   6. _____
7. When you are at the (1)**P.O.** (2)**post office,** will you please buy some stamps for me?   7. _____
8. He worked for the J. C. Penney (1)**Company** (2)**Co.** for ten years.   8. _____
9. She will tour Germany, (1)**Eng.** (2)**England,** and France next summer.   9. _____
10. Robert Bailey, (1)**M.D.** (2)**medical doctor,** is my physician.   10. _____
11. Frank jumped 22 feet, (1)**3** (2)**three** inches in last Saturday's meet.   11. _____
12. I had purchased coffee, flour, sugar, (1)**etc.** (2)**and other groceries.**   12. _____
13. He had made a dental appointment for (1)**3** (2)**three** o'clock.   13. _____
14. It was necessary for him to leave the campus by 2 (1)**P.M.** (2)**o'clock.**   14. _____
15. John's yearly income was (1)**$14,640** (2)**fourteen thousand six hundred forty dollars.**   15. _____
16. She graduated from high school on June (1)**6** (2)**6th,** (3)**sixth,** 1984.   16. _____
17. He and his family moved to Vermont last (1)**Feb.** (2)**February,** didn't they?   17. _____
18. Over (1)**900** (2)**nine hundred** students attend Roosevelt Junior High School.   18. _____
19. She was late in getting to her (1)**phys. ed.** (2)**physical education** class.   19. _____
20. Next year's convention will be held on April (1)**19,** (2)**19th,** (3)**nineteenth,** in Burlington.   20. _____
21. The petition contained (1)**2,983** (2)**two thousand nine hundred eighty-three** names.   21. _____
22. The lottery prize has reached an astonishing (1)**twenty-four million dollars.** (2)**$24 million.**   22. _____
23. Our neighbor had adopted a (1)**two-month-old** (2)**2-month-old** baby boy.   23. _____
24. (1)**The Reverend Harold Olson** (2)**Rev. Olson** was the speaker.   24. _____
25. The diagram was on (1)**pg.** (2)**page 44.**   25. _____
26. Mrs. Latimer will teach (1)**English** (2)**Eng.** next semester at Lowell High School.   26. _____
27. Jody bought a puppy at the SPCA for (1)**Xmas.** (2)**Christmas.**   27. _____
28. I found the chart on page (1)**two hundred forty-one** (2)**241** very helpful.   28. _____
29. The plane expected from (1)**L.A. early this** A.M. (2)**Los Angeles early this morning** is late.   29. _____
30. The bus arrives at 10:55 A.M. and leaves at (1)**11:00** (2)**eleven** A.M.   30. _____

31. Ben earned (1)*three hundred dollars* (2)*$300,* saved $80, and spent $40.   31. _____

32. Rachel's name was (1)*twenty-sixth* (2)*26th* on the list of high school graduates.   32. _____

33. The bad roads meant I had to use (1)*4-* (2)*four-*wheel drive.   33. _____

Name _____ Class _____ Date _____ Score (R _____ × 4) _____

66. MECHANICS: CAPITALS, NUMBERS, AND ABBREVIATIONS

(Study M-2, M-4, and M-5.)

In the first column, write the number of the **first correct** choice (**1** or **2**).
In the second column, write the number of the **second correct** choice (**3** or **4**).

Example: There are only (1)*three* (2)*3* more days until (3)*Summer* (4)*summer* vacation.   _1_ _4_

1. Racial attitudes of many South African (1)*White* (2)*white* people must change if everyone there is to enjoy full (3)*Civil Rights.* (4)*civil rights.*   1. ___ ___
2. We have an (1)*Aborigine* (2)*aborigine* from Australia studying (3)*Engineering* (4)*engineering* here.   2. ___ ___
3. My (1)*Aunt* (2)*aunt* said her job was "(3)*Super* (4)*super* terrific."   3. ___ ___
4. "I expect," he said, "(1)*To* (2)*to* get an A in my (3)*Chem.* (4)*chemistry* class."   4. ___ ___
5. On June (1)*6* (2)*6th,* 1982, she spoke at St. Paul's (3)*High School.* (4)*high school.*   5. ___ ___
6. The new college (1)*President* (2)*president* greeted the (3)*Alumni.* (4)*alumni.*   6. ___ ___
7. An (1)*american* (2)*American* flag flies from the top of the Empire State (3)*building* (4)*Building.*   7. ___ ___
8. The (1)*treasurer* (2)*Treasurer* of the (3)*Junior Accountants Club* (4)*junior accountants club* has absconded with our dues.   8. ___ ___
9. (1)*308* (2)*Three hundred eight* students passed the test, out of (3)*427* (4)*four hundred twenty-seven* who took it.   9. ___ ___
10. She likes her (1)*english* (2)*English* and (3)*science* (4)*Science* classes.   10. ___ ___
11. We knew that (1)*spring* (2)*Spring* in all her beauty would soon be smiling on the hills of eastern (3)*nebraska* (4)*Nebraska.*   11. ___ ___
12. Industry in the (1)*South* (2)*south* is described in this month's (3)*Fortune* (4)*fortune* magazine.   12. ___ ___
13. Victor is going to take an (1)*english* (2)*English* course this semester instead of one in (3)*History.* (4)*history.*   13. ___ ___
14. She was happy; (1)*She* (2)*she* had reservations on the (3)*lurline.* (4)*Lurline.*   14. ___ ___
15. The new (1)*doctor* (2)*Doctor* has opened an office on Main (3)*Street.* (4)*street.*   15. ___ ___
16. The (1)*chinese* (2)*Chinese* student is (3)*18* (4)*eighteen* years old today.   16. ___ ___
17. I spent (1)*New Year's Day* (2)*new year's day* with (3)*mother.* (4)*Mother.*   17. ___ ___
18. Her (1)*French* (2)*french* teacher is going to the (3)*Orient.* (4)*orient.*   18. ___ ___
19. I need a (1)*Psychology* (2)*psychology* book from the (3)*Library.* (4)*library.*   19. ___ ___
20. The (1)*class* (2)*Class* of '75 honored the (3)*Dean of Men.* (4)*dean of men.*   20. ___ ___
21. Carla enrolled in (1)*Doctor* (2)*Dr.* Newell's history course; she is majoring in (3)*social science.* (4)*Social Science.*   21. ___ ___
22. Jim moved to eastern Montana; (1)*He* (2)*he* bought over (3)*400* (4)*four hundred* acres of land.   22. ___ ___

23. She knows (1)*four* (2)*4* students who are going to (3)*College* (4)*college* this fall.   23. _____ _____

24. The election of a (1)*Republican* (2)*republican* President precipitated the Civil (3)*War.*
    (4)*war.*   24. _____ _____

25. After WW II, many (1)*blacks* (2)*Blacks* moved away from the rural parts of the (3)*South.*
    (4)*south.*   25. _____ _____

Name _____ Class _____ Date _____ Score (R _____ × ¾) _____

67. SPELLING: RECOGNIZING CORRECT FORMS

(Study S-1.)

Write the number of the **correctly spelled** word.

Example: A knowledge of (1)*grammer* (2)*grammar* is helpful.   2

1. (1)*Athletics* (2)*Atheletics* can be both healthful and enjoyable.   1. _____
2. I'm glad you didn't take it (1)*personaly.* (2)*personally.*   2. _____
3. No one thought that a romance would (1)*develope* (2)*develop* between those two.   3. _____
4. Your snapshot will never come out; the sun is (1)*shining* (2)*shinning* into your lens.   4. _____
5. Shakespeare's Iago is one of the classic (1)*villains* (2)*villians* of the stage.   5. _____
6. There are sins of commission and sins of (1)*ommission.* (2)*omission.*   6. _____
7. Her grandmother will be (1)*ninety* (2)*ninty* years old next week.   7. _____
8. The salary will depend on how (1)*competant* (2)*competent* the employee is.   8. _____
9. We (1)*persued* (2)*pursued* the pickpocket through the crowd.   9. _____
10. We canceled our plans because of the (1)*changeable* (2)*changable* summer weather.   10. _____
11. He offered several (1)*ridiculous* (2)*rediculous* excuses for his behavior.   11. _____
12. Her car will (1)*accomodate* (2)*accommodate* only five passengers.   12. _____
13. Americans can be proud of our (1)*achievements* (2)*achievments* in space exploration.   13. _____
14. Do you (1)*beleive* (2)*believe* everything that you read in the newspaper?   14. _____
15. My husband and I are fortunate in having (1)*similar* (2)*similiar* tastes.   15. _____
16. She is an (1)*unusually* (2)*unusualy* gifted musician, isn't she?   16. _____
17. Carrying automobile insurance seems a (1)*necessary* (2)*neccessary* precaution.   17. _____
18. I find you strangely (1)*desirable.*(1)*desireable.*   18. _____
19. His (1)*couragous* (2)*courageous* act won for him much admiration from the associates.   19. _____
20. She is (1)*optomistic* (2)*optimistic* about her chances of passing the course.   20. _____
21. Despite Holmes' warning, Scotland Yard once more let Moriarity (1)*disappear* (2)*dissappear* from London.   21. _____
22. I had already (1)*payed* (2)*paid* my tuition for the fall semester.   22. _____
23. My adviser (1)*reccomended* (2)*recommended* my enrolling in an English course.   23. _____
24. Her future (1)*happiness* (2)*happyness* was very important to him.   24. _____
25. Two hunting (1)*knifes* (2)*knives* had been stolen from the trophy case.   25. _____
26. To be praised extravagantly always (1)*embarrasses* (2)*embarasses* him.   26. _____
27. (1)*Repitition* (2)*Repetition* can easily become very monotonous.   27. _____
28. I had (1)*fulfilled* (2)*fullfilled* all the requirements for graduation.   28. _____
29. Because he was overly (1)*agressive* (2)*aggressive* he was not very popular.   29. _____
30. She was eager to (1)*receive* (2)*recieve* an A in the course.   30. _____

109

31. Vanessa was left to make the final (1)*arrangments* (2)*arrangements* for the funeral. 31. _____
32. I would have (1)*profited* (2)*profitted* greatly by taking his advice. 32. _____
33. He is (1)*occasionally* (2)*ocassionally* absent from class. 33. _____
34. I was sitting in my room when the incident (1)*occured* (2)*occurred* in the lobby. 34. _____
35. The work of Dian Fossey demonstrates that gorillas have more than just a (1)*primitive* (2)*primative* intelligence. 35. _____
36. The spelling errors in her paper were very (1)*noticable.* (2)*noticeable.* 36. _____
37. The school (1)*superintendent* (2)*superintendant* visited several classes. 37. _____
38. The (1)*principle* (2)*principal* introduced him to several of the teachers. 38. _____
39. The coach said, "Live tackling will (1)*seperate* (2)*separate* the men from the boys." 39. _____
40. What a great (1)*athlete* (2)*athelete* he is! 40. _____
41. She tried (1)*dying* (2)*dyeing* some of her sweaters another color. 41. _____
42. Little Jonathan is now going to (1)*kindegarten.* (2)*kindergarten.* 42. _____
43. Is it too late to save our (1)*enviroment?* (2)*environment?* 43. _____
44. She was (1)*disappointed* (2)*disapointed* about the outcome of the election. 44. _____
45. His (1)*sternness* (2)*sterness* seemed completely uncalled for. 45. _____
46. An (1)*undisceplined* (2)*undisciplined* childhood probably explained his wildness. 46. _____
47. Her lack of interest had become very (1)*apparent* (2)*apparant* to all of us. 47. _____
48. I suggest you find a good (1)*phychologist* (2)*psychologist* immediately. 48. _____
49. The arbitrator's solution seemed (1)*sensible,* (2)*sensable.* 49. _____
50. The (1)*sophomore* (2)*sophmore* class voted to sponsor a dance next month. 50. _____
51. The high school's star athlete was a very (1)*conscientous* (2)*conscientious* student. 51. _____
52. After school each day, he washed dishes in a downtown (1)*restaurant.* (2)*restuarant.* 52. _____
53. Thanks to my word processor, I never (1)*misspell* (2)*mispell* words. 53. _____
54. The (1)*occurrence* (2)*occurence* was reported in the student newspaper. 54. _____
55. He annoyed her by keeping time to the (1)*rythm* (2)*rhythm* of the music. 55. _____
56. I could only guess at the age and (1)*heigth* (2)*height* of the giant redwood tree. 56. _____
57. He earned extra money by repairing (1)*radios* (2)*radioes* during the summer. 57. _____
58. Filling out (1)*questionaires* (2)*questionnaires* proved to be very time-consuming. 58. _____
59. Robert's (1)*perseverance* (2)*perseverence* led to his ultimate success in the theater. 59. _____
60. She has a (1)*tendancy* (2)*tendency* to do her best work early in the day. 60. _____
61. Carla put the dress back, refusing to pay the (1)*outragious* (2)*outrageous* price. 61. _____
62. Her services had become (1)*indispensible* (2)*indispensable* to the firm. 62. _____
63. A reception was held for students having an (1)*excellent* (2)*excellant* scholastic record. 63. _____
64. Steven patiently explained the (1)*mathamatics* (2)*mathematics* of the experiment to me, but I was still lost. 64. _____
65. You will find no (1)*prejudice* (2)*predjudice* in our organization. 65. _____
66. The farmer was dependent on (1)*government* (2)*goverment* subsidy. 66. _____

67. (1)*Professor* (2)*Proffessor* Hacksaw won't accept late papers. 67. _____
68. We were told to (1)*proceed* (2)*procede* with our experiment. 68. _____
69. Nobody (1)*tries* (2)*trys* harder than Wilbur to be a good basketball player. 69. _____
70. Haven't you (1)*ommitted* (2)*omitted* the name of the club president? 70. _____
71. Too many (1)*unecessary* (2)*unnecessary* digressions spoiled the speech. 71. _____
72. Caldwell is (1)*suppose to* (2)*supposed to* deliver the lumber some time today. 72. _____
73. You can say (1)*potatos* (2)*potatoes* two ways but spell it only one. 73. _____
74. The aging movie actress still imagined herself to be (1)*irresistible.* (2)*irresistable.* 74. _____
75. A minor accident occurred in the chemistry (1)*labratory.* (2)*laboratory.* 75. _____
76. It was always a (1)*priviledge* (2)*privilege* to listen to her talk. 76. _____
77. An (1)*erroneous* (2)*erronous* announcement appeared in the local newspaper. 77. _____
78. His (1)*curiosity* (2)*curiousity* led him into new areas of research. 78. _____
79. The king's son was completely bald; still, everyone said he was the heir (1)*aparent.* (2)*apparent.* 79. _____
80. Only (1)*amateur* (2)*amatuer* athletes may compete in this event. 80. _____

Name _____ Class _____ Date _____ Score (R _____ × 1%) _____

68. SPELLING: CORRECTING ERRORS

(Study S-1 and S-2.)

Twenty of the words below are misspelled (in addition to the sample).
After each **correct** word, write **1** in the narrow column and nothing in the wide column.
After each **misspelled** word, write **0** in the narrow column and the correct spelling in the wide column.

Example: hindrance   1
Example: vacum   0   vacuum

1. tragedy
2. writing
3. anxious
4. definite
5. proceedure
6. neice
7. wierd
8. familiar
9. acknowlege
10. maneuver
11. possession
12. comparitive
13. truly
14. mischievious
15. prevalent
16. preceeding
17. auxiliary
18. conceivable
19. irresistible
20. permissable
21. sacrilegious
22. millionnaire
23. independent
24. character
25. adolescense
26. acquainted
27. nucleus
28. pastime
29. catagory
30. fourty
31. amateur
32. foreign
33. business
34. prejudice
35. nineth
36. entirely
37. finally
38. sergeant
39. persistant
40. parallel
41. acquire
42. percieve
43. synonym
44. ectasy
45. argument
46. exaggerate
47. knowledge
48. exciteable

49. exhilaration _____ _____
50. dissatisfied _____ _____
51. eighth _____ _____
52. maintenence _____ _____
53. existence _____ _____
54. playwright _____ _____

55. hindrance _____ _____
56. schedule _____ _____
57. written _____ _____
58. management _____ _____
59. rhythm _____ _____
60. reminise _____ _____

69. SPELLING: CORRECTING ERRORS

(Study S-1 and S-2.)

On each line, **one** of the three words is misspelled.
In the narrow blank, write the column number of the **misspelled** word.
In the wide blank, write the misspelled word **correctly**.

Column 1	Column 2	Column 3	Number of Column Containing Misspelled Word	Misspelled Word Written Correctly
Example: definate	opinion	ridiculous	1	definite
1. surprise	guarantee	perserverence		
2. forty	discription	condemn		
3. criticism	comparitively	anxious		
4. millionaire	indispensible	prevalent		
5. acquired	pursue	auxillary		
6. acknowledge	wierd	fictitious		
7. apparant	maneuver	dropping		
8. occurred	restaurant	changable		
9. exaggerate	recieve	maintenance		
10. ninty	ninth	foreign		
11. argument	curiousity	separate		
12. sensable	erroneous	shining		
13. dilemma	tendency	questionaire		
14. usually	sophmore	mischievous		
15. priviledge	pastime	perform		
16. forcibly	omission	exhileration		
17. fasinating	government	reminisce		
18. superintendent	intelligence	hypocricy		
19. ecstasy	kindergarten	occurence		
20. existance	perceive	omitted		

21. synonym   sacrilegous   vengeance   _____ _____
22. vacuum   noticable   amateur   _____ _____
23. outrageous   unnecesary   repetition   _____ _____
24. optimistic   dissatisfied   accomodate   _____ _____
25. strength   tradgedy   sophomore   _____ _____
26. misspelled   loveless   aquainted   _____ _____
27. sieze   acquitted   adolescence   _____ _____
28. irrelevant   primative   villain   _____ _____
29. aggressive   knowlege   height   _____ _____
30. writing   possession   competant   _____ _____

70. SPELLING: WORDS FREQUENTLY MISSPELLED

(Study S-2.)

In the numbered blank, write the number of the **letter missing** in the word: **1** for **a**, **2** for **e**, **3** for **i**, **4** for **o**. If **no letter is missing,** write **0**.

Example: gramm r   1   21. math matics   21. ____

1. ben fited   1. ____   22. pre judice   22. ____
2. tend ncy   2. ____   23. consist nt   23. ____
3. occurr nce   3. ____   24. prim tive   24. ____
4. pleas nt   4. ____   25. prev lent   25. ____
5. defin te   5. ____   26. compar tive   26. ____
6. permiss ble   6. ____   27. rep tition   27. ____
7. opt mistic   7. ____   28. nec ssary   28. ____
8. believ ble   8. ____   29. sacrileg ous   29. ____
9. d scription   9. ____   30. compet nt   30. ____
10. d vide   10. ____   31. desp rate   31. ____
11. lov ble   11. ____   32. superintend nt   32. ____
12. sim lar   12. ____   33. exist nce   33. ____
13. appar nt   13. ____   34. excell nt   34. ____
14. hindr nce   14. ____   35. sep rate   35. ____
15. d spair   15. ____   36. independ nt   36. ____
16. lab ratory   16. ____   37. irresist ble   37. ____
17. indispens ble   17. ____   38. persever nce   38. ____
18. famil ar   18. ____   39. opp rtunity   39. ____
19. argu ment   19. ____   40. priv lege   40. ____
20. forc bly   20. ____

In the numbered blank,
write **1** if the missing letters are *ie;*
write **2** if the missing letters are *ei.*

Example: gr f   1   6. v n   6. ____
1. h r   1. ____   7. ch f   7. ____
2. ach ve   2. ____   8. l sure   8. ____
3. dec ve   3. ____   9. th r   9. ____
4. c ling   4. ____   10. w gh   10. ____
5. w rd   5. ____   11. shr k   11. ____

116

12. r gn
13. bes ge
14. n ther
15. n ce
16. conc ve

12. _____
13. _____
14. _____
15. _____
16. _____

17. conc t
18. rec ve
19. bel ve
20. fr nd

17. _____
18. _____
19. _____
20. _____

Name _____ Class _____ Date _____ Score (R ___ × 3, + 1) ___

71. USAGE: WORDS SIMILAR IN SOUND

(Study U.)

Write the number of the **correct** choice.

Example: (1) *Your* (2) *You're* lovelier than ever.   __2__

1. Take my (1)*advice* (2)*advise,* Julius; stay home today.   1. ____
2. I felt (1)*alright* (2)*all right* until I ate the soup.   2. ____
3. If you (1)*break* (2)*brake* the car gently, you won't feel a jolt.   3. ____
4. Camping trailers with (1)*canvas* (2)*canvass* tops are cooler than hardtop trailers.   4. ____
5. The diamond Richard bought for Elizabeth weighed more than three (1)*carets.* (2)*carats.*   5. ____
6. The cost of their (1)*cloths* (2)*clothes* would bankrupt a millionaire.   6. ____
7. The sandpaper was too (1)*course* (2)*coarse* for the job.   7. ____
8. Helping Allie with calculus was quite a (1)*decent* (2)*descent* gesture, don't you agree?   8. ____
9. This little (1)*device* (2)*devise* will revolutionize the computer industry.   9. ____
10. The new milk-pricing regulations angered the (1)*diary* (2)*dairy* industry.   10. ____
11. To (1)*elicit* (1)*illicit* student response, the teacher may ask affective as well as cognitive questions.   11. ____
12. She was one of the most (1)*imminent* (2)*eminent* educators of the decade.   12. ____
13. We knew that enemy troops would try to (1)*envelop* (2)*envelope* us.   13. ____
14. Kevin (1)*formerly* (2)*formally* had pitched for the Phillies.   14. ____
15. Go (1)*fourth* (2)*forth,* youngsters, and conquer the world.   15. ____
16. I hate to (1)*hear* (2)*here* what the dean is going to report.   16. ____
17. Sir, your notion is (1)*irrelevant* (2)*irreverent* to the issue.   17. ____
18. The ferry made the trip to the (1)*aisle* (2)*isle* in less than an hour.   18. ____
19. She tried vainly to (1)*lessen* (2)*lesson* the tension in the house.   19. ____
20. The mourners wept as they filed (1)*passed* (2)*past* the bier.   20. ____
21. Morality is never simply a matter of (1)*personal* (2)*personnel* taste.   21. ____
22. The (1)*piece* (2)*peace* of the plane fell off in mid-flight.   22. ____
23. Her (1)*presents* (2)*presence* makes this a gala occasion.   23. ____
24. When the grand marshal gave the signal, the parade (1)*preceded.* (2)*proceeded.*   24. ____
25. Some people forsake the city to enjoy a (1)*quiet* (2)*quite* country life.   25. ____
26. Consider getting your degree as a (1)*rite* (2)*right* of passage.   26. ____
27. You can buy typing paper at any (1)*stationary* (2)*stationery* store.   27. ____
28. They knew better (1)*than* (2)*then* we did what the answer was.   28. ____
29. We caught a train that went (1)*thorough* (2)*through* to Manchester.   29. ____
30. After weeks of miserable (1)*whether,* (2)*weather,* Scott gave up and went home.   30. ____

31. She is the first (1)*woman* (2)*women* to umpire in this league. 31. _____

32. (1)*Your* (2)*You're* aware, aren't you, that the play is sold out? 32. _____

33. This dot-matrix printer will (1)*complement* (2)*compliment* your computer. 33. _____

Name _____ Class _____ Date _____ Score (R _____ × 10/9) _____

72. USAGE: WORDS SIMILAR IN SOUND

(Study U.)

Write the number of the **correct** choice.

Example: William is (1)*to* (2)*too* (3)*two* clever for his own good.   __2__

1. The rulers of the planet Zarkon will (1)*advice* (2)*advise* Earthlings not to land there.   1. _____
2. She signed the letter, "(1)*Respectively* (2)*Respectfully* yours."   2. _____
3. It is never (1)*all right* (2)*alright* for a driver to pass a stop sign.   3. _____
4. This handbag should (1)*complement* (2)*compliment* your new suit perfectly.   4. _____
5. Ned should be careful not to (1)*lose* (2)*loose* his temper so often.   5. _____
6. Go (1)*fourth* (2)*forth* and sin no more, the Bible says.   6. _____
7. I'd rather be right (1)*then* (2)*than* President.   7. _____
8. The (1)*course* (2)*coarse* for the marathon includes both flat and hilly terrain.   8. _____
9. Knowing that they have sufficient funds will (1)*lesson* (2)*lessen* their financial worries.   9. _____
10. The spectators fled when Marshall picked up the (1)*discuss.* (2)*discus.*   10. _____
11. Nobody (1)*accept* (2)*except* Gloria would stoop so low.   11. _____
12. If you write such things in your (1)*diary,* (2)*dairy,* keep it locked away.   12. _____
13. You will not find a better (1)*women* (2)*woman* on the entire staff.   13. _____
14. If you don't eat your spinach, Fiona, you won't get (1)*desert.* (2)*dessert.*   14. _____
15. She yearned for (1)*peace* (2)*piece* and tranquility in her daily life.   15. _____
16. If he (1)*past* (2)*passed* the physics test, it must have been easy.   16. _____
17. Ronald Reagan (1)*preceded* (2)*proceeded* George Bush as President.   17. _____
18. The library copy of the magazine had lost (1)*it's* (2)*its* cover.   18. _____
19. He made his way (1)*thorough* (2)*through* the heavy underbrush.   19. _____
20. We had (1)*already* (2)*all ready* made arrangements to travel by bus.   20. _____
21. Can you name the (1)*capitols* (2)*capitals* of the fifty states in the United States?   21. _____
22. I'm certain that (1)*your* (2)*you're* not intending to miss the concert tonight.   22. _____
23. His physical condition showed the (1)*effects* (2)*affects* of adequate rest and good food.   23. _____
24. I wouldn't try to (1)*prophecy* (2)*prophesy* what his future will be.   24. _____
25. We were (1)*quite* (2)*quiet* pleased with the results of our experiment.   25. _____
26. The steep (1)*descent* (2)*decent* down the mountain road was very hazardous.   26. _____
27. Shall we dress (1)*formally* (2)*formerly* for the Senior Ball this year?   27. _____
28. To be a good teacher had become her (1)*principal* (2)*principle* concern.   28. _____
29. Are you certain that the bracelet is made of ten-(1)*carrot* (2)*caret* (3)*carat* gold?   29. _____

120

30. The Farkle family were (1)*altogether* (2)*all together* in the living room when their good friend and trusted neighbor made his surprise announcement. 30. _____
31. Shall I read the statement that (1)*precedes* (2)*proceeds* the examination questions? 31. _____
32. Would it not be better to make the dog's collar (1)*loser?* (2)*looser?* 32. _____
33. "I, (1)*too* (2)*to* (3)*two* have a statement to make," she said. 33. _____
34. The bridge club stared in horror as the creature made (1)*its* (2)*it's* way toward them. 34. _____
35. The high-school (1)*principle* (2)*principal* spoke at the opening assembly. 35. _____
36. He said, "(1)*Their* (2)*There* (3)*They're* is no reason for you to wait." 36. _____
37. I could scarcely (1)*hear* (2)*here* what was being said because of the noise outside. 37. _____
38. "(1)*Whose* (2)*Who's* there?" she whispered hoarsely. 38. _____
39. "(1)*Accepting* (2)*Excepting* this award," she sobbed, "is an honor I deserve." 39. _____
40. They wanted a house with a separate (1)*dinning* (2)*dining* room. 40. _____
41. I decided to discuss my problem with the (1)*personnel* (2)*personal* manager. 41. _____
42. She had made up her mind to buy a new suit of (1)*cloths.* (2)*clothes.* 42. _____
43. The mere (1)*cite* (2)*sight* (3)*site* of Juliet made his heart soar. 43. _____
44. I hope to install a (1)*device* (2)*devise* that will serve as a burglar alarm. 44. _____
45. The new teacher was asked to (1)*consul* (2)*counsel* (3)*council* thirty-five students. 45. _____
46. I was willing to pay 6 percent interest on the unpaid (1)*principle.* (2)*principal.* 46. _____
47. His words were vulgar and his manners (1)*course.* (2)*coarse.* 47. _____
48. Lay your books on the table; (1)*then* (2)*than* we'll make plans for the evening. 48. _____
49. Will people be standing in the (1)*isles* (2)*aisles* at the dedication ceremony? 49. _____
50. Parts of the document were immaterial and (1)*irrelevant.* (2)*irreverent.* 50. _____
51. "Sad movies always (1)*effect* (2)*affect* me this way," he said laughing. 51. _____
52. She could not decide (1)*whether* (2)*weather* or not to go back to work. 52. _____
53. The president suggested a (1)*canvas* (2)*canvass* of the members of the organization. 53. _____
54. He was obviously (1)*effected* (2)*affected* by the beauty of his surroundings. 54. _____
55. As children, we played a game to see who could stand (1)*stationary* (2)*stationery* for the longest time. 55. _____
56. I (1)*complimented* (2)*complemented* him on his extraordinary presence of mind. 56. _____
57. He is very (1)*through* (2)*thorough* and painstaking in all that he does. 57. _____
58. Jonathan had the (1)*presence* (2)*presents* of mind to make a sharp right turn and step on the accelerator. 58. _____
59. They started out alone on a dreary trip across the (1)*dessert.* (2)*desert.* 59. _____
60. This was another (1)*instance* (2)*instants* of his kindness and generosity. 60. _____
61. Two (1)*woman* (2)*women* and two men were on the committee. 61. _____
62. Dr. McBride is a distinguished and (1)*eminent* (2)*imminent* member of the faculty. 62. _____
63. We were (1)*already* (2)*all ready* to go on the pony ride when the rains came. 63. _____
64. The teacher had reported the matter to the (1)*principal.* (2)*principle.* 64. _____
65. It's obvious that (1)*there* (2)*they're* (3)*their* unwilling to listen to reason. 65. _____

66. The measure passed without a (1)*fourth* (2)*forth* of the arguments' being presented. 66. _____
67. I was certain that he would not (1)*desert* (2)*dessert* the ship. 67. _____
68. The track coach told me that he wanted to (1)*discus* (2)*discuss* my performance at the last meet. 68. _____
69. The moving object had now become (1)*stationary.* (2)*stationery.* 69. _____
70. "What is (1)*you're* (2)*your* candid opinion?" she asked. 70. _____
71. "(1)*Who's* (2)*Whose* your friend in the yellow car?" he asked. 71. _____
72. In the mountains we quickly felt the (1)*affects* (2)*effects* of a change in elevation. 72. _____
73. She was very (1)*clothes* (2)*close* to winning when she withdrew from competition. 73. _____
74. Her attitude was impertinent and (1)*irreverent.* (2)*irrelevant.* 74. _____
75. We suspected that an upset in our plans was (1)*eminent.* (2)*imminent.* 75. _____
76. The class (1)*prophesy* (2)*prophecy* was read by the president of the Senior Class. 76. _____
77. Come (1)*forth* (2)*fourth* and you won't win any medals. 77. _____
78. I could never (1)*quite* (2)*quiet* understand her motives. 78. _____
79. In later life, Toto was appointed honorary (1)*council* (2)*consul* (3)*counsel* for the Land of Oz. 79. _____
80. "(1)*You're* (2)*Your* most certainly wrong!" he exclaimed. 80. _____

Name _____ Class _____ Date _____ Score (R _____ × 1%) _____

73. USAGE: WORD CHOICE

(Study U.)

Write the number of the **correct** choice. (Formal standard English is intended.)

Example: Willa wanted the doll very (1)*much.* (2)*badly.*   __1__

1. He keeps trying to (1)*discover* (2)*invent* a better mousetrap.   1. _____
2. Your essay has (1)*its* (2)*it's* faults, but it makes some excellent points too.   2. _____
3. A tall tree has fallen and is (1)*laying* (2)*lying* across the highway.   3. _____
4. The exhaust fumes made him feel (1)*nauseated* (2)*nauseous.*   4. _____
5. In *The Oxbow Incident*, the wrong man is (1)*hung.* (2)*hanged.*   5. _____
6. I could not help (1)*but feel* (2)*feeling* sad when I read the book.   6. _____
7. Did you ask if he will (1)*let* (2)*leave* you open a charge account?   7. _____
8. She thought that she had paid (1)*to* (2)*too* (3)*two* much for her television set.   8. _____
9. I found that the bag of potatoes had (1)*busted* (2)*burst* (3)*bursted* open.   9. _____
10. We were surprised (1)*somewhat* (2)*some* at his sudden outburst.   10. _____
11. The old inn is only a short (1)*ways* (2)*way* down the road.   11. _____
12. Will the new legislation (1)*affect* (2)*effect* your business enterprise?   12. _____
13. I really should'nt have (1)*excepted* (2)*accepted* his generous offer of help.   13. _____
14. We were (1)*real* (2)*very* pleased they came to the rodeo.   14. _____
15. You and Michael will have to share the book (1)*between* (2)*among* you.   15. _____
16. We heard the same report (1)*everywhere* (2)*everyplace* we went.   16. _____
17. I knew that it would be (1)*alright* (2)*all right* for us to go the matinee.   17. _____
18. That the people are sovereign is the first (1)*principle* (2)*principal* of a democratic society.   18. _____
19. As soon as he had (1)*affected* (2)*effected* his release, he telephoned her.   19. _____
20. Do (1)*try to* (2)*try and* spend the night with us when you are in town.   20. _____
21. I suspected that Sue's mother was (1)*most* (2)*almost* at the end of her patience.   21. _____
22. "Shooting innocent civilians is one of war's most (1)*amoral* (2)*immoral* acts," the minister said.   22. _____
23. The alfalfa milkshake may taste awful, but it is (1)*healthy.* (2)*healthful.*   23. _____
24. Sarah always (1)*lies* (2)*lays* down to rest after an unusual exertion.   24. _____
25. Timothy (1)*lay* (2)*laid* new linoleum on the floor of the recreation room last week.   25. _____
26. (1)*As for me* (2)*As for my part,* I particularly dislike television commercials.   26. _____
27. My reading stories (1)*aloud* (2)*out loud* delighted the children.   27. _____
28. When my dog wants (1)*in* (2)*to come in,* she barks and whines.   28. _____
29. I went (1)*right* (2)*directly* to the cafeteria after my last class.   29. _____
30. The (1)*amount* (2)*number* of trees needed to produce a single book should humble any author.   30. _____

31. We were (1)*altogether* (2)*all together* satisfied with the arrangements.   31. _____
32. I shall withhold judgment until his statements are (1)*proven* (2)*proved* untrue.   32. _____
33. The Allies scheme was (1)*practicable* (2)*practical* but dangerous.   33. _____
34. I (1)*had ought* (2)*ought* to have let her know the time of my arrival.   34. _____
35. They had (1)*already* (2)*all ready* canceled their reservations.   35. _____
36. The dog has (1)*laid* (2)*lain* on the front steps all morning.   36. _____
37. Caroline is an (1)*alumnus* (2)*alumna* of UCLA.   37. _____
38. *Chokies* taste good (1)*like* (2)*as* a carcinogen should.   38. _____
39. She (1)*suspected* (2)*suspicioned* her dog of having stolen the package of meat.   39. _____
40. He (1)*adopted* (2)*adapted* readily to a change in his environment.   40. _____
41. She was not (1)*enthused* (2)*enthusiastic* about his plan to buy a ranch.   41. _____
42. Will you be sure to (1)*contact* (2)*get in touch with* me tomorrow?   42. _____
43. He (1)*seldom ever* (2)*hardly ever* writes to his sister.   43. _____
44. Anna was (1)*besides* (2)*beside* herself with anger.   44. _____
45. (1)*Hadn't I ought* (2)*Ought I not* to report the incident at once?   45. _____
46. Buck is throwing the ball (1)*good* (2)*well* this spring.   46. _____
47. Do (1)*set* (2)*sit* down and tell me all about your summer vacation.   47. _____
48. The man was (1)*annoyed* (2)*aggravated* by the noise made by his neighbor's children.   48. _____
49. I believe that she is living (1)*someplace* (2)*somewhere* in South America.   49. _____
50. One reason for his poor health is (1)*because* (2)*that* he doesn't get enough sleep.   50. _____
51. The curtain was about to (1)*raise* (2)*rise* on the last act of the senior play.   51. _____
52. He exclaimed, "I (1)*couldn't hardly* (2)*could hardly* believe my ears!"   52. _____
53. She lived in constant fear of (1)*losing* (2)*loosing* her passport.   53. _____
54. Mother was (1)*sure* (2)*surely* happy when I told her that I would be home for Christmas.   54. _____
55. Exhausted from their cold plunge into the ocean, the swimmers were (1)*laying* (2)*lying* on the beach.   55. _____
56. The camp is just a few miles (1)*further* (2)*farther* along this trail.   56. _____
57. I wrote to the registrar (1)*in regard to* (2)*in regards to* my missing transcript.   57. _____
58. The passengers were instructed to fasten (1)*they're* (2)*their* (3)*there* seat belts.   58. _____
59. Judge Bean sentenced Black Bart to be (1)*hanged* (2)*hung* immediately after the trial.   59. _____
60. She wanted (1)*badly* (2)*very much* to stay in Japan for a month of sightseeing.   60. _____

74. USAGE: WORD CHOICE

(Study U.)

Write **1** if the boldface expression is **correct**.
Write **0** if it is **incorrect**.
(Formal standard English is intended.)

Example: The car's fender was dented and ***it's*** windshield was cracked.   0

1. ***Those sort*** of books are expensive.   1. ____
2. He played ***like*** he was inspired.   2. ____
3. Standards of living have ***raised***.   3. ____
4. Some dogs look ***like*** their masters.   4. ____
5. You ***hadn't ought*** to sneak into the show.   5. ____
6. ***It's*** time for us to go.   6. ____
7. You ***too*** can afford such a car.   7. ____
8. We were ***plenty*** surprised at the outcome.   8. ____
9. I couldn't find John ***anyplace.***   9. ____
10. He parked his car ***in back of*** Deborah's house.   10. ____
11. The cornerstone was being ***laid.***   11. ____
12. ***Irregardless*** of the result, you did your best.   12. ____
13. Will he ***raise*** your salary?   13. ____
14. Try to keep him ***off of*** the pier.   14. ____
15. I ***suspicioned*** him of dishonesty.   15. ____
16. He ***rarely ever*** arrives late.   16. ____
17. Just try ***and*** stop me!   17. ____
18. Her success was ***due to*** hard work and persistence.   18. ____
19. I'm to go too, ***aren't I?***   19. ____
20. ***They're*** house is now for sale.   20. ____
21. Julia and ***myself*** decided to open a dress shop.   21. ____
22. The club has lost ***its*** president.   22. ____
23. Susan is ***awfully*** happy.   23. ____
24. Did he ***lay*** awake last night?   24. ____
25. She is not ***enthused*** about tennis.   25. ____
26. Bob ***laid*** the carpet in the hallway.   26. ____
27. We ***sure*** hope you are able to go.   27. ____
28. He ***better*** get here before noon.   28. ____
29. She is a ***real*** reliable person.   29. ____
30. He ***has been laying*** in the hammock all morning.   30. ____
31. I admire ***that kind*** of initiative.   31. ____
32. He has ***plenty*** of opportunities for earning money.   32. ____
33. He was ***plenty*** worried at not hearing from her.   33. ____
34. David looked ***like*** he wanted to avoid her.   34. ____
35. ***Most*** all her friends sent cards.   35. ____
36. The damage was ***nowhere near*** as great as I thought it might be.   36. ____
37. He always did ***good*** in English.   37. ____
38. She resigned ***because of*** illness.   38. ____
39. He ***lay*** in bed until noon.   39. ____
40. Max has ***less*** enemies than Sam.   40. ____
41. He ***laid*** his hammer on the porch.   41. ____
42. He has a long ***way*** to go tonight.   42. ____
43. Did he ***loose*** his wallet?   43. ____
44. She walked ***like*** she was in pain.   44. ____
45. He told the dog to ***lay*** down.   45. ____
46. Who were the ***principals*** in the company?   46. ____
47. His finances are in bad ***shape.***   47. ____
48. Have you written ***in regards to*** an appointment?   48. ____
49. Elaine ***adopted*** her novel for television.   49. ____
50. Damp weather ***affects*** her sinuses.   50. ____

125

| Name _____ Class _____ Date _____ Score (R _____ × 1%) _____ |

75. USAGE: WORD CHOICE

(Study U.)

Write the number of the **correct** choice. (Formal standard English is intended.)

Example: Fix it (1)*anyways* (2)*any way* you can.   __2__

1. The book's author was (1)*censored* (2)*censured* for his views.   1. _____
2. You may borrow (1)*any one* (2)*anyone* of my books if you promise to return it.   2. _____
3. Compared (1)*to* (2)*with* the Redskins, the Raiders have a weaker defense but a stronger offense. 3. _____
4. The figure of Venus de Milo is an excellent example of (1)*classic* (2)*classical* sculpture. 4. _____
5. He should (1)*of* (2)*have* notified his hostess of his change in plans.   5. _____
6. The linebacking unit was (1)*composed* (2)*comprised* of Taylor, Marshall, and Burt.   6. _____
7. Be (1)*sure to* (2)*sure and* write to us when you arrive in Massachusetts.   7. _____
8. They invited no one to their wedding (1)*except* (2)*accept* their parents.   8. _____
9. (1)*Regardless* (2)*Irregardless* of difficulties, he will complete the project.   9. _____
10. The reason I changed my mind was (1)*because* (2)*that* she was persistent.   10. _____
11. The referee was completely (1)*uninterested* (2)*disinterested* and completely dedicated. 11. _____
12. The three children tried to outrun (1)*each other.* (2)*one another.*   12. _____
13. Early rainstorms had (1)*raised* (2)*risen* the level of the lake.   13. _____
14. (1)*Everyplace* (2)*Everywhere* we went, we encountered hospitable people.   14. _____
15. He is very (1)*enthusiastic* (2)*enthused* about playing the part of the villain.   15. _____
16. I spoke to the agent about (1)*ensuring* (2)*insuring* the cottage.   16. _____
17. I'm a very stupid person, (1)*aren't I* (2)*am I not* (3)*ain't I*?   17. _____
18. We could not ship by air the (1)*number* (2)*amount* of cartons that the company ordered. 18. _____
19. The vase was (1)*setting* (2)*sitting* on the table where I had left it.   19. _____
20. Her brilliant performance was (1)*due to* (2)*because of* talent and ability.   20. _____
21. Bob and (1)*myself* (2)*I* will spend the summer in New England.   21. _____
22. Man's first step on the moon was a (1)*historic* (2)*historical* moment in the exploration of space. 22. _____
23. We had (1)*less* (2)*fewer* problems than we had anticipated.   23. _____
24. When the playground director arrived, Tom was (1)*nowheres* (2)*nowhere* to be found.   24. _____
25. The teenagers spent the day (1)*laying* (2)*lying* on the beach in the sun.   25. _____
26. If you (1)*lose* (2)*loose* your driver's license, report the loss at once.   26. _____
27. He followed directions just (1)*like* (2)*as* he had been instructed.   27. _____
28. (1)*Due to* (2)*Because of* uncertain weather, our flight had been canceled.   28. _____
29. He was put on probation (1)*due to* (2)*because of* habitual truancy.   29. _____
30. A (1)*rising* (2)*raising* barometer indicated a marked change in the weather.   30. _____

31. The child's body showed obvious (1)*effects* (2)*affects* of malnutrition. 31. _____
32. The quick snack he had before dinner (1)*lessoned* (2)*lessened* his hunger. 32. _____
33. The new ruling will (1)*affect* (2)*effect* all entering students this fall. 33. _____
34. The statue (1)*sits* (2)*sets* on a high pedestal opposite the entrance to the park. 34. _____
35. I walked (1)*past* (2)*passed* her without speaking. 35. _____
36. The loud ticking of the clock proved to be very (1)*aggravating* (2)*annoying* to her. 36. _____
37. A cloud of smoke was (1)*rising* (2)*raising* from the distant hillside. 37. _____
38. Detective Chandler gave the apartment a (1)*through* (2)*thorough* inspection. 38. _____
39. The leader's efforts to find them had been (1)*altogether* (2)*all together* praiseworthy. 39. _____
40. People considered him a man of high (1)*principles.* (2)*principals.* 40. _____
41. Excuse me, Your Honor, but I have to (1)*utilize* (2)*use* the bathroom. 41. _____
42. Her attitude toward the problem was quite different (1)*from* (2)*than* his. 42. _____
43. He (1)*could hardly* (2)*couldn't hardly* make his way up the steep incline. 43. _____
44. The test was (1)*not nearly* (2)*nowhere near* as difficult as she expected it to be. 44. _____
45. He receives (1)*less* (2)*fewer* telephone calls than I do. 45. _____
46. She wanted to believe that there was (1)*no such a* (2)*no such* word as *can't*. 46. _____
47. We had no doubt (1)*but what* (2)*that* he would one day become a college president. 47. _____
48. I shall let you know our decision (1)*within* (2)*inside of* an hour. 48. _____
49. The doctors worked feverishly to remove the (1)*piece* (2)*peace* of shrapnel from the infantryman's leg. 49. _____
50. The rank of captain in the navy corresponds (1)*to* (2)*with* that of colonel in the army. 50. _____
51. Let the documents (1)*lie* (2)*lay* on the table where he left them. 51. _____
52. We invited (1)*the Reverend Mr. Englund* (2)*Reverend Englund* to come as our guest. 52. _____
53. The speakers were much better informed about the subject (1)*then* (2)*than* I was. 53. _____
54. I am very late in handling in this paper, (1)*aren't I?* (2)*am I not?* 54. _____
55. My inability to pay was (1)*due to* (2)*because of* a shortage of funds. 55. _____
56. I, (1)*to,* (2)*too,* was in agreement with the speaker's remarks about the controversy. 56. _____
57. She was (1)*very much* (2)*plenty* upset about her low scholastic average. 57. _____
58. He was obviously (1)*two* (2)*to* (3)*too* stunned to speak. 58. _____
59. (1)*Any more* (2)*Anymore* behavior like that, young man, and you'll go straight to bed. 59. _____
60. Shouldn't you (1)*lay* (2)*lie* down after your long walk? 60. _____

| Name _____ | Class _____ | Date _____ | Score (R _____ × 2) _____ |

76. USAGE: WORD CHOICE

(Study U.)

Write **1** if the boldface expression is **correct**.
Write **0** if it is **incorrect**.
(Formal standard English is intended.)

Example: The day was *like* a bad dream. 1

1. A lion hunting its prey is *immoral.* 1. ___
2. The bus was *already* to leave. 2. ___
3. They *normally always* win. 3. ___
4. Has *any one* here seen Betty? 4. ___
5. *Almost* all my friends came. 5. ___
6. The hum of the air conditioner was *continual.* 6. ___
7. The villain is usually *hanged.* 7. ___
8. The car runs *good* now. 8. ___
9. She is *too* young to understand. 9. ___
10. *Irregardless* of his shortcomings, she loves him. 10. ___
11. Where is my bankbook *at*? 11. ___
12. He had no intention of jumping *off of* the bridge. 12. ___
13. The salesperson *contacted* him. 13. ___
14. The sun will *hopefully* shine tomorrow. 14. ___
15. *They're* financial obligations had become too heavy for them. 15. ___
16. The harshness of his voice proved *irritating* to me. 16. ___
17. His chances looked *good.* 17. ___
18. The twins frequently wear *one another's* clothes. 18. ___
19. A twisted branch was *laying* across our path. 19. ___
20. She was *disinterested* in the boring play. 20. ___
21. Minerva was *enthused* about being on the basketball team. 21. ___
22. The auditorium holds *less* then six hundred people. 22. ___
23. The conflicting groups finally *effected* a compromise. 23. ___
24. Kate was *somewhat* annoyed. 24. ___
25. Sam *differs from* Gina about the need for more taxes. 25. ___
26. I meant to *lay* down for an hour. 26. ___
27. Let's think *further* about it. 27. ___
28. What are you looking *at*? 28. ___
29. He enjoys the *healthy* food we serve. 29. ___
30. The children had walked to school by *theirselves.* 30. ___
31. I could not help *but feel* sorry for the two culprits. 31. ___
32. Her story was *incredulous.* 32. ___
33. It is a *most unique* situation. 33. ___
34. He had *already* departed. 34. ___
35. Theirs was a *lose* arrangement. 35. ___
36. *Due to* the pollution levels, the city banned incinerators. 36. ___
37. The three girls chatted with *each other* about the party. 37. ___
38. First and second honors were given to John and Harold, *respectively.* 38. ___
39. I was *mad* with love for her. 39. ___
40. Only Alex and *myself* attended the meeting. 40. ___
41. She was *terribly* pleased at winning the contest. 41. ___
42. *Their* is always another game. 42. ___
43. The red rug had *lain* on the floor for ten years. 43. ___
44. Let's hope the vote will be sooner *then* later. 44. ___
45. Foyt *lead* the race from start to finish. 45. ___

128

46. He *implied* that I was at fault.   46. _____
47. *Lie* down your heavy load.   47. _____
48. The cost of living keeps *rising.*   48. _____
49. *They're* not at home today.   49. _____
50. We ventured *further* into the woods.   50. _____

77. USAGE: WORD CHOICE

(Study U.)

Write **1** if the boldface expression is **correct**.
Write **0** if it is **incorrect**.
(Formal standard English is intended.)

Example: Malina **sure** could sew.   0

1. Two of the pirates were **hanged.** 1. ___
2. The child seemed to be **healthy.** 2. ___
3. She died **due to** pneumonia. 3. ___
4. Jaime **emigrated** from Mexico in 1988. 4. ___
5. The phone rang **continually.** 5. ___
6. We leave **inside** of five minutes. 6. ___
7. The dig reached the bottom **strata.** 7. ___
8. His reasons are different **than** mine. 8. ___
9. I was **continually** interrupted. 9. ___
10. **Being as** I was early, I waited. 10. ___
11. He bought cake, soda, **and etc.** 11. ___
12. June has **less** days than July. 12. ___
13. Be **sure and** write if you get work. 13. ___
14. He hiked **farther** than I. 14. ___
15. Swimming is **healthful** exercise. 15. ___
16. They **seldom ever** meet. 16. ___
17. He lost **due to** inexperience. 17. ___
18. It took more than an hour to **climb up** Mount Abraham. 18. ___
19. I **set** my packages on the table. 19. ___
20. Eli Whitney **discovered** the cotton gin. 20. ___
21. Her **folks** will be here tomorrow. 21. ___
22. I shall **contact** my attorney. 22. ___
23. He faltered **because of** fatigue. 23. ___
24. He fell **off** the ladder. 24. ___
25. I am **nowhere near** ready to go. 25. ___
26. Sue's balloon had **bursted.** 26. ___
27. The temple **sits** on a high hill. 27. ___

28. I **can but** sympathize with him. 28. ___
29. I asked **in regards to** my check. 29. ___
30. I am **enthused** about this job. 30. ___
31. Biff is a **hardy-type** fellow. 31. ___
32. I **see where** the school bonds failed to pass. 32. ___
33. The reason she stutters is **because** she's nervous. 33. ___
34. He **cannot help but** be grateful for the help he has received. 34. ___
35. The cat has been **lying** on the hearth all afternoon. 35. ___
36. I'm sure that he will be **O.K.** 36. ___
37. The instructor's lack of comments **aggravated** her. 37. ___
38. He **rose** petunias as a hobby. 38. ___
39. She does **well** in examinations. 39. ___
40. The red dress looks **good** on her. 40. ___
41. Dr. Freud remained **mad** for years. 41. ___
42. I looked **everyplace** for my pen. 42. ___
43. Dillinger was a **notable** public enemy. 43. ___
44. I **laid** my purse on the counter. 44. ___
45. The class was **all together** bored by the film. 45. ___
46. No modern playwright can be **compared to** Shakespeare. 46. ___
47. All roads lead there. Take **anyone.** 47. ___
48. When offered beer and wine, I choose the **latter.** 48. ___
49. We will **except** you from the rule. 49. ___
50. Is this test **verbal** or written? 50. ___

Name _____ Class _____ Date _____ Score (R _____ × 5) _____

78. USAGE: WORD CHOICE

(Study U.)

Write **1** if the sentence is **correct**.
Write **0** if the sentence is **incorrect**; then write the correct version of the misused word in the second column.

Example: Its been a unique experience.   0   It's

1. Some people drive their cars like everyone else on the road were a sworn enemy.   1. ___ ___
2. We were altogether surprised when little Brian decided to take a nap.   2. ___ ___
3. There were far less campers at Camp Walletmaker that summer than its bunkhouses could hold.   3. ___ ___
4. We wanted to lay in the sun for a week and work on our tans.   4. ___ ___
5. Being jolted by 50 volts had little apparent affect on Harold, who insisted it had brightened up his day.   5. ___ ___
6. They laid the new floor in the kitchen in less than a day.   6. ___ ___
7. Parker said it was alright with him to put anchovies on the pizza but implied that he was just being polite.   7. ___ ___
8. Irregardless of my grades, I'm an excellent writer, except for word usage.   8. ___ ___
9. Keep your principles and you'll seldom ever regret it.   9. ___ ___
10. Making usage errors is truly aggravating, especially when someone cites an authority to prove you are wrong.   10. ___ ___
11. I sometimes lose track of the time when I am besides a beautiful thing.   11. ___ ___
12. We were far too credible about the investment, and that's how we lost our capital.   12. ___ ___
13. He better get to class on time; Professor Morrison is apt to complain if he's late again.   13. ___ ___
14. The judge was uninterested; she wished to determine only if the complaint were a genuine instance of discrimination.   14. ___ ___
15. Your absolutely right to go to traffic court and dispute the ticket.   15. ___ ___
16. Providing that she doesn't lose sight of her objective, she's a good bet to make the team.   16. ___ ___
17. When we saw that the restaurant was a little further down the road, our morale greatly improved.   17. ___ ___
18. Lie your head on my shoulder so that you can rest.   18. ___ ___
19. This sort of fish is far more tastier than any other.   19. ___ ___
20. We were far too close to the refineries; I began to feel nauseous.   20. ___ ___

Name _____ Class _____ Date _____ Score (R _____ × 12 + 4) _____

79. BEYOND THE SENTENCE: PARAGRAPH DEVELOPMENT

(Study B-1.)

Underline the **topic sentence** of each paragraph. Then, in the blank at the end of the paragraph, write the number of the **method** used to develop the topic sentence:

1. **facts or examples**
2. **reasons**
3. **definition**
4. **comparison or contrast**

1. Every society tries to produce a prevalent psychological type that will best serve its ends, and that type is always prone to certain emotional malfunctions. In early capitalism, which was a producing society, the ideal type was acquisitive, fanatically devoted to hard work and fiercely repressive of sex. The emotional malfunctions to which this type was liable were hysteria and obsession. Later capitalism, today's capitalism, is a consuming society, and the psychological type it strives to create, in order to build up the largest possible markets, is shallow, easily swayed and characterized much more by self-infatuation than self-respect. The emotional malfunction of this type is narcissism.
—Margaret Halsey   1. _____

2. Now, to be properly enjoyed, a walking tour should be gone upon alone. If you go in a company, or even in pairs, it is no longer a walking tour in anything but name; it is something else and more in the nature of a picnic. A walking tour should be gone upon alone, because freedom is of the essence; because you should be able to stop and go on, and follow this way and that, as the freak takes you; and because you must have your own pace, and neither trot alongside a champion walker, nor mince in time with a girl. And then you must be open to all impressions and let your thoughts take color from what you see. You should be as a pipe for any wind to play upon. "I cannot see the wit," says Hazlitt, "of walking and talking at the same time. When I am in the country, I wish to vegetate like the country"—which is the gist of all that can be said upon the matter. There should be no cackle of voices at your elbow to jar on the meditative silence of the morning. And so long as a man is reasoning he cannot surrender himself to that fine intoxication that comes of much motion in the open air, that begins in a sort of dazzle and sluggishness of the brain, and ends in a peace that passes comprehension.
—Robert Louis Stevenson   2. _____

3. If you have any doubt of what a word means, look it up. Learn its etymology and notice what curious branches its original root has put forth. See if it has any other meanings that you didn't know it had. Master the small gradations between words which seem to be synonyms. What is the difference between "cajole," "wheedle," "blandish," and "coax"? An excellent guide to these nuances is *Webster's Dictionary of Synonyms*.
—William Zinsser   3. _____

4. The most essential distinction between athletics and education lies in the institution's own interest in the athlete as distinguished from its interest in its other students. Universities attract students in order to teach them what they do not already know; they recruit athletes only when they are already proficient. Students are educated for something which will be useful to them and to society after graduation; athletes are required to spend their time on activities the usefulness of which disappears upon graduation or soon thereafter. Universities exist to do what they can for students; athletes are recruited for what they can do for the universities. This makes the operation of the athletic program in which recruited players are used basically different from an educational interest of colleges and universities.
—Harold W. Stoke   4. _____

5.   Any education that matters is *liberal*. All the saving truths and healing graces that distinguish a good education from a bad one or a full education from a half-empty one are contained in that word. Whatever ups and down the term *"liberal"* suffers in the political vocabulary, it soars above all controversy in the educational world. In the blackest pits of pedagogy the squirming victim has only to ask, "What's liberal about this?" to shame his persecutors. In times past a liberal education set off a free man from a slave or a gentleman from laborers and artisans. It now distinguishes whatever nourishes the mind and spirit from the training which is merely practical or professional or from trivialities which are not training at all. Such an education involves a combination of knowledge, skills, and standards.
—Alan Simpson   5. _____

6.   The fictional urge is basic. Humans dream in stories, daydream in stories; express hope for the future, account for the present, and recapture the past in stories. Fictional literature is an extension of life. It begins in tale telling, assumes widely divergent forms in different times and cultures, feeds upon itself in imitation or rejections of its constantly changing past, and takes specific shape in the print of an individual work.
—Northrop Frye   6. _____

7.   What, then, is thinking? To begin with, it is a purposeful mental activity over which we exercise some control. *Control* is the key word. Just as sitting in the driver's seat of a car becomes driving only when we take the steering wheel in hand and control the car's movement, so our mind's movements become thinking only when we direct them.
—Vincent Ryan Ruggiero   7. _____

8.   A cognitive science project weaves together three strands of research activity: theory development, empirical research, and model building. Each of these activities has far less impact in isolation from the other two. *Theory development* elaborates the set of constructs from which empirical research and model building take their impetus; the theory guides the experiment and forms the basis for the model. *Empirical research* validates and constrains the theory and determines the parameters of the working model. *Model building* instantiates and extends the theory and generates new hypotheses that need to be tested empirically.
—Jon M. Slack   8. _____

Name _____ Class _____ Date _____ Score (R _____ × 20) _____

80. BEYOND THE SENTENCE: PARAGRAPH DEVELOPMENT WITH SPECIFICS

(Study B-1.)

<u>Underline</u> the **topic sentence** in each paragraph. In addition

write **1** in the blank at the end if the paragraph develops its topic sentence adequately **and** then write another sentence that would continue its development.
write **0** if the paragraph is not adequately developed **and** then write the reason why you think so.

1. Young people today see how their parents feel and act. Since they feel that their parents are wrong, they rebel because they do not want to become carbon copies of their elders. Young people want to be treated as people, not just children who do not know what they are talking about and who should therefore not express their own ideas. Young people today want to do and think as they please. They do not want their ideas to be pushed aside for an older person's ideas. They want a free society where there is nothing that they must do because it is required of them. They want to experience new and different things. Whatever their elders want, they do the opposite so as not to be like them. 1. _____

2. Today's athletes are overpaid. Although it is undeniable that not everyone can toss a basketball through a hoop or throw a baseball ninety miles an hour, that doesn't mean that fans should have to pay the admission prices they do. People who like sports have other ways to spend their money, such as movies or vacations. Some of them can't even afford to go to sporting events. Doctors and nurses also perform valuable services to society; should they be rich enough to retire at thirty-five? The cost of living for the average person continues to climb. Athletes should not be millionaires, no matter how talented they are. 2. _____

3. Bob Kennedy's public speeches invariably exhorted action—especially action by the young or for the young. It was with the young that both men enjoyed a special rapport. John Kennedy was the youngest man ever elected President. He surrounded himself with young aides and young advisers. He offered youth an opportunity to serve—in the Peace Corps, in Washington internships, in the ghetto. His programs stressed the next generation and his style as well as his age appealed to them and made them feel represented, that someone was listening to their gripes. His death created a vacuum that only RFK could fill.
—Theodore C. Sorensen 3. _____

4. The study found that collection crews spent only a small portion of their day picking up garbage. Crews observed in Manhattan spent an average of two hours and 55 minutes at it, while those in Brooklyn collected garbage for three hours and 22 minutes a day, and crews in Staten Island worked on collection for three hours and 33 minutes a day.
—Josh Barbanel 4. _____

5. I like the old movies shown on TV better than the ones shown in theaters in recent years. The old films contain plots that are more dramatic and actors that are more famous. Such films are exciting and fast-paced. The actors are widely known for their acting ability. Today's films often drag and have less famous actors. 5. _____

81. BEYOND THE SENTENCE: PARAGRAPH UNITY

(Study B-1.)

Underline the **topic sentence** of each paragraph. Then, in the blanks at the end of the paragraph, write the number(s) of any sentence(s) in the paragraph that **do not relate directly** to the topic sentence.

1. ¹From a pebble on the shore to a boulder on a mountainside, any rock you see began as something else and was made a rock by the earth itself. ²Igneous rock began as lava that over hundreds of years hardened far beneath the earth's surface. ³Granite is an igneous rock. ⁴Sedimentary rock was once sand, mud, or clay that settled to the bottom of a body of water and was packed down in layers under the ocean floor. ⁵All rocks are made up of one or more minerals. ⁶Metamorphic rock began as either igneous rock or sedimentary rock whose properties were changed by millions of years of exposure to the heat, pressure, and movement below the earth's crust.

    1. _____

2. ¹Although we normally associate suits of armor with the knights of medieval Europe, the idea of such protective coverings is much older and more pervasive than that. ²Some knights even outfitted their horses with metal armor. ³As long as 3500 years ago, Assyrian and Babylonian warriors sewed pieces of metal to their leather tunics the better to repel enemy arrows. ⁴A thousand years later, the Greeks wore metal helmets, in addition to large metal sheets over their chests and backs. ⁵Native Americans of the Northwest wore both carved wooden helmets and chest armor made from wood and leather. ⁶Nature protects the turtle and the armadillo with permanent armor. ⁷Even with body armor largely absent from the modern soldier's uniform, the helmet still remains as a reminder of the vulnerability of the human body.

    2. _____

3. ¹Computers have forever changed the way we work. ²Clerks no longer add rows of numbers by hand. ³Writers are freed of keeping pages and pages of documentation on their shelves. ⁴Many persons fear that computers will take away jobs. ⁵Computer-controlled robots have changed the way factories manufacture everything from cars to toys. ⁶There is always the danger of misusing the computer, such as by storing personal information about people. ⁷Someone has even programmed a computer to flip hamburgers.

    3. _____

4. ¹I'd much rather read a book than see a movie. ²When you read, you can imagine for yourself what characters look like and how they sound. ³You can pick up a book at any time and not have to line up for a film to begin. ⁴It is true, however, that you can do the same with videos. ⁵A book goes with you to be read anywhere—you never have to be in a specific place. ⁶When you find a passage you like, you can reread it or just pause and think about things. ⁷Of course, it's always fun to be in a theater with other people.

    4. _____

82. BEYOND THE SENTENCE: PARAGRAPH COHERENCE—TRANSITIONS

(Study B-1.)

For each item, choose from the list the **transitional expression** that fits most logically in the space. Then write the number of that expression (**1** to **10**) in the blank at the right. (For some items there is more than one possible answer.)

1. Afterward
2. Consequently
3. Even so
4. Formerly
5. However
6. Meanwhile
7. Nevertheless
8. On the other hand
9. That is
10. Therefore

Example: I think, _____, I am.   _10_

1. The night of the prom, we danced every step we knew. _____, we strolled on the moonlit beach.

2. There is widespread agreement that females can do virtually any job. _____, there are still many questions about the effect this may have on the relationships between men and women.

3. The pony express was far faster than any previous mail service to the far West. _____, with the Civil War threatening, the 250-miles-per-day pace of the riders was too slow for Western newspaper editors and their readers.

4. I am terminating my periodic disbursement to you. _____, I am cutting off your allowance.

5. As the nobles bickered among themselves as to who should station themselves at defensive positions and who should counterattack, the king spent increasingly more time with his astrologers. _____, the rebels marched closer to the capital.

6. A person speaking to members of his or her own family uses language that is informal and intimate. A person speaking to a large group, _____, is likely to choose different words and a different tone of voice.

7. If you toss a coin repeatedly and it comes up heads each time, common sense tells you to expect tails to turn up soon. _____, the chances of heads coming up remain the same for each toss of the coin.

8. Today, computers are inexpensive enough to put in virtually every office and in every school. _____, the cost of such machines was prohibitive.

9. In general, a small animal acclimatizes better than a large one. _____, the small animal finds it easier to adjust to changes in the environment.

10. It was evident to the foreperson and to the other jurors that they were hopelessly deadlocked. _____, the foreperson sent word to the judge that they were unable to agree on a verdict.

A List of Grammatical Terms

The following chart gives brief definitions, examples, and nonexamples of the grammatical terms you'll read about most often in these exercises. Refer to *English Simplified* for more information.

Term	What It *Is* or *Does*	Examples	Nonexamples
Adjective	Describes a noun	a *fast* runner (describes the noun **runner**)	He runs **fast** (describes the verb runs)
Appositive	A noun that renames another	Tom Wolfe, **the writer,** lives in New York. (The appositive follows the man's name).	**Tom Wolfe,** the writer, lives in New York.
Adverb	Describes a verb, adjective, or another adverb	He runs **fast** (describes the verb **run**) He runs **very** fast (describes the adverb **fast**) He is an **extremely** fast runner (describes the adjective **fast**)	He is a **fast** runner. (Here, **fast** is an adjective.)
Clause	A group of words with a subject and a predicate. A *main clause* can stand by itself and make complete sense; a *dependent clause* must be attached to a main clause.	*He is a fast runner.* (A main clause) *if he is a fast runner* (A dependent clause that must be attached to some main clause; for example, *he would win.*)	a **fast runner** (merely a noun and its adjective)
Complement	Completes the meaning of the verb.	Direct Object: He threw the **ball.** (Says what got thrown.) Indirect Object: He threw the ball to **me.** (Says who benefited by the ball being thrown.) Subjective Complement: He is a **pitcher.** (Renames the subject **He** after the linking verb **is.**) Objective Complement: The team named Rodgers **coach.** (Follows the direct object **Rodgers** and renames it.)	**He** threw the ball. (Says who did the action rather than received it.)
Conjunction	A word that joins.	Coordinating conjunction: Joins things of equal importance: Boys **and** girls. Poor **but** honest. Subordinating Conjunction: Joins a dependent clause to a main clause: I left **when** she arrived.	I left **at** noon. (**At** is a preposition.)
Fragment	A group of words that cannot stand by themselves and make complete sense.	**when I saw them** (a dependent clause) **from Maine to California** (a prepositional phrase)	**They went from Maine to California.** (A main clause that can stand by itself.)

Term	What It *Is* or *Does*	Examples	Nonexamples
Noun	Names a person, place, animal, or thing.	***Tom Denver cat book***	***throw*** (a verb) ***red*** (an adjective)
Phrase	A group of words without a subject and a verb.	***from California*** (a prepositional phrase) ***to see the king*** (an infinitive phrase) ***built of bricks*** (a participial phrase) ***building houses*** (a gerund phrase)	***He is from California.*** (a main clause)
Predicate	The part of the sentence that speaks about the subject.	The man ***threw the ball.*** (Says what the subject did.)	The ***man*** threw the ball. (The ***man*** performed the action.)
Pronoun	A word that replaces a noun.	***He*** will be here soon. (***He*** takes the place of the man's name.)	***Jonathan*** will be here soon. (***Jonathan*** is a noun.)
Subject	The person or thing about whom the sentence speaks.	***Polly*** writes children's books.	Polly ***writes children's books.*** (***Writes children's books*** is the predicate, that is, the action she performs.)
Verb	Says what the subject either *does* or *is*.	She ***buys*** seashells. She ***is*** smart.	***Emily*** is smart. (***Emily*** is a noun.)

Teaching-Learning Aid
DIAGRAMING

Diagraming is a method of analyzing sentences and of visually depicting parts of speech and their functions in sentences. Though diagrams can grow complex, their basic principle is simple: Everything in the complete subject is written to the left of the main vertical line; everything in the complete predicate, to the right. All the main parts of a sentence are written on or above the main horizontal line; all the secondary parts, below the main horizontal line.

Simple sentence

An old friend from school often sends me very funny postcards.

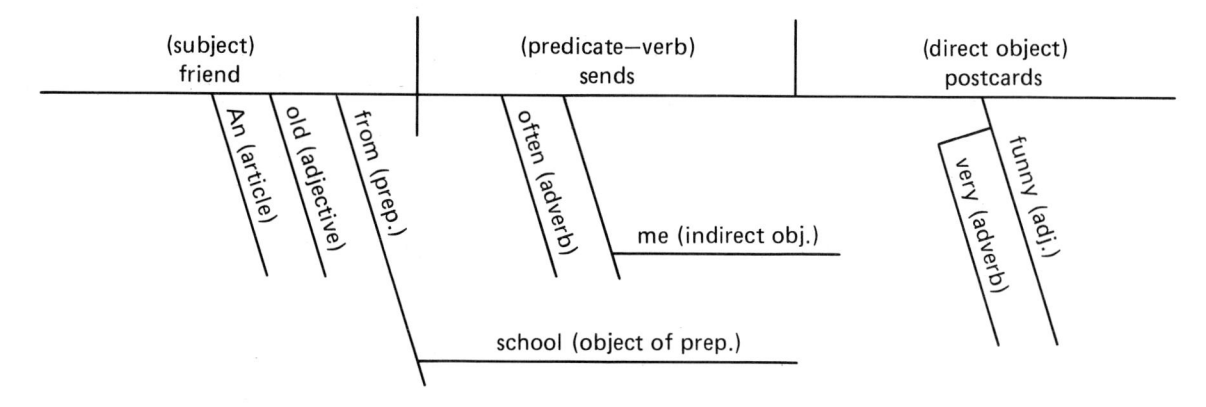

Simple sentence with compound parts

Romeo and Juliet fell in love and planned a secret wedding.

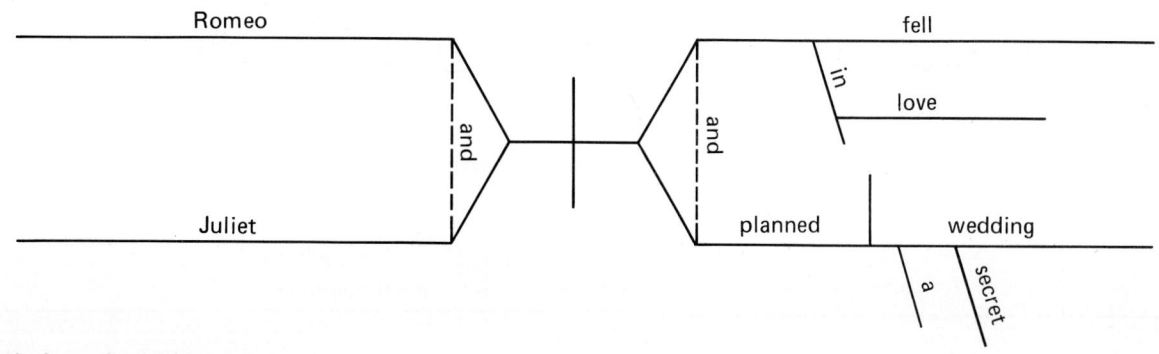

Verbals and verbal phrases

Used as modifiers

Reeling under our attacks (participial phrase), the *decimated* (participle) enemy requested a truce *to arrange a surrender* (infinitive phrase).

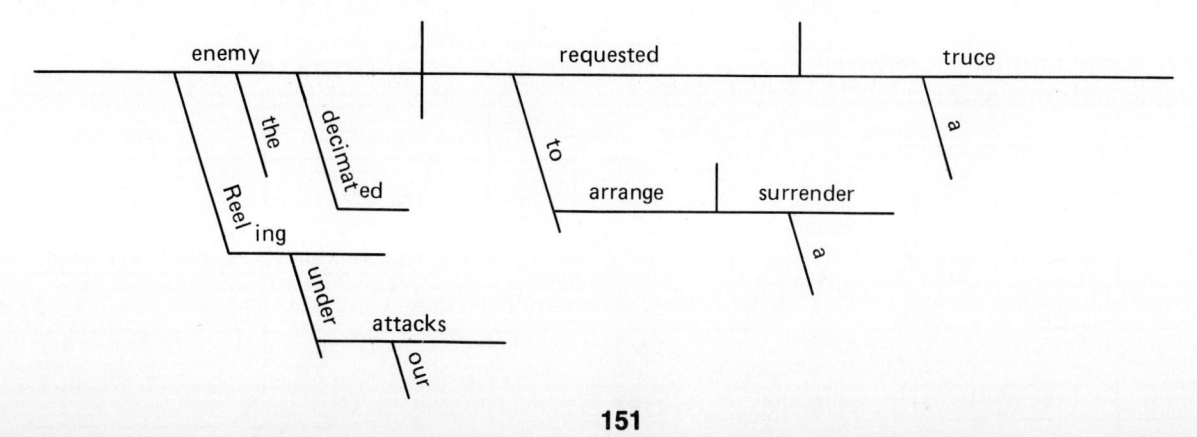

Verbals and verbal phrases

Used as nouns

They denied *having tried to embezzle funds by falsifying data.* (Italicized words are a gerund phrase; within that phrase are an infinitive phrase, *to embezzle funds*, and another gerund phrase, *falsifying data.*)

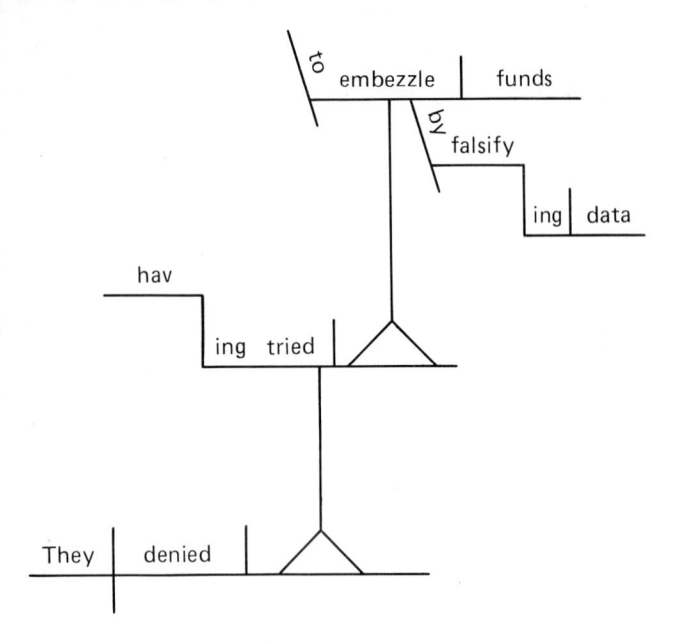

Compound sentence

We tried hard, but we failed badly.

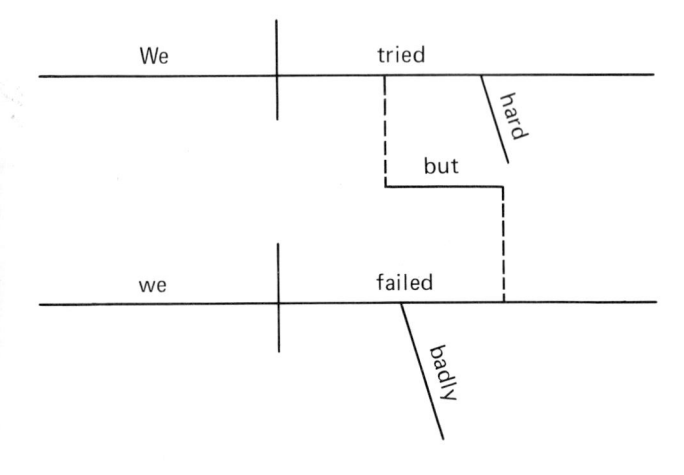

Complex sentence

With adjective clause (dotted line between relative pronoun and antecedent)

I respect a person *who can resist pressure.*

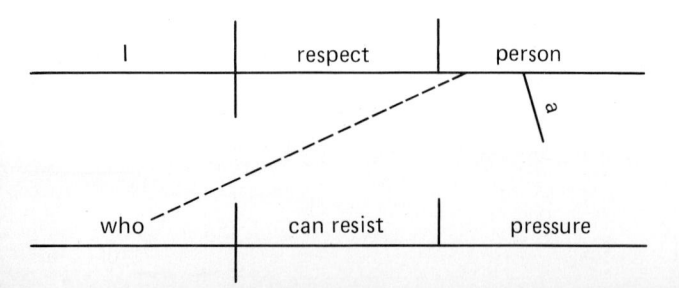

Complex sentence

With adverb clause (dotted line between verb of adverb clause and word the clause modifies)

We will continue our campaign *until we make Jones mayor.*

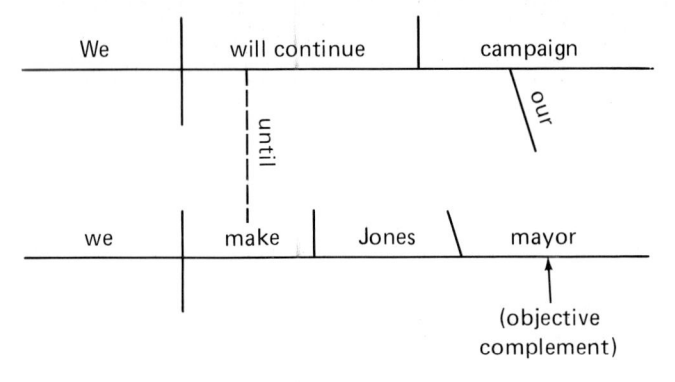

With noun clause (on tower)

You should take *whatever you can get.*

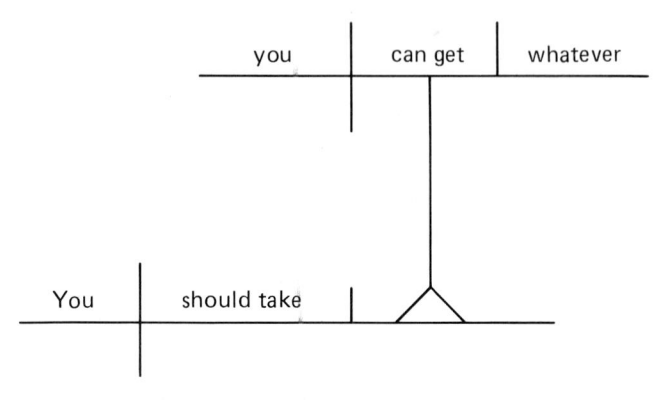

That you will succeed is almost certain.

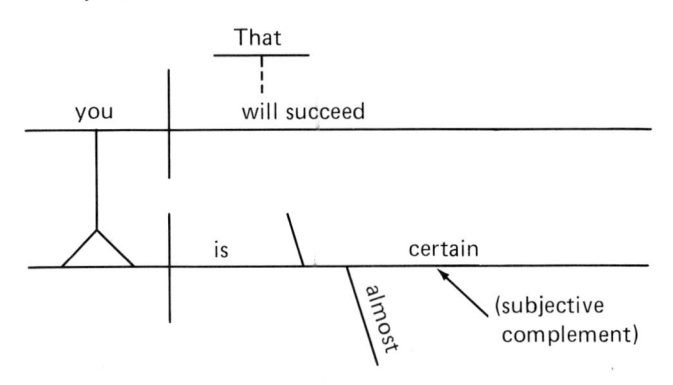

Give it to *whoever answers the door.*

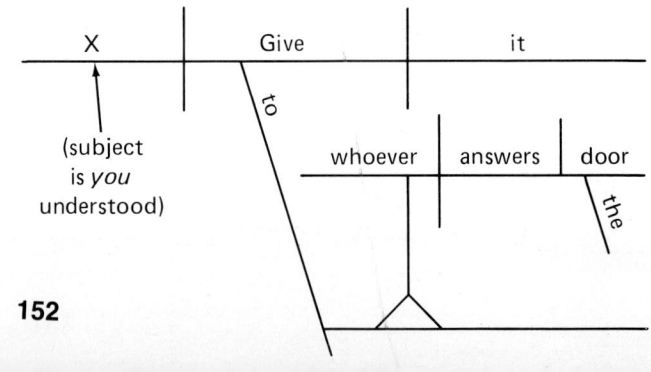

(subject is *you* understood)

152